SUSHI AT HOME

SUSHI AT HOME

A Mat-to-Table Sushi Cookbook

ROCKRIDGE
PRESS

CONTENTS

INTRODUCTION

Sitting down to a meal at a sushi bar is an engaging experience for the eyes and the palate alike. Before you lies an array of colorful fish ready to be sliced by the sushi master's sharp knife. The nose breathes in the briny aroma of fish and shellfish fresh from the sea; the tongue delights at the clean, salty, sweet, and umami flavors. Then, of course, comes the shock when the bill arrives to remind you of all the beautiful, aromatic, and delicious sushi you were unable to resist. But what if you could make sushi at home? You could treat yourself to the captivating experience of a sushi bar without overspending, while still impressing your friends (and yourself) at the same time. Perhaps more than any other cuisine, sushi inspires its fans to go beyond merely consuming it (at every possible opportunity!) to also learn about its history, cultural significance, intricate rules, and dizzying range of flavors and textures that make sushi so addicting. The idea of making the Japanese dish at home may feel intimidating at first. After all, don't sushi masters have to train for years before they are allowed behind the sushi bar?

It's true that becoming a Japanese master sushi chef takes a long time, but once you understand and become familiar with the basic techniques, becoming a proficient home sushi chef is much simpler than you might imagine. The key to making sushi without creating chaos in your kitchen is simple: Prepare your fillings and toppings ahead of time, and organize your workspace so that when it comes time to make the sushi, it is a matter of assembly.

Arguably the most challenging, and certainly the most essential, part of making sushi is getting the rice just right. The step-by-step instructions in this book guide you through the process—first by showing you how to choose the right type of rice (available at most grocery stores and online), and then by instructing you in how to prepare, cook, season, and cool the rice to achieve the perfect balance of flavor and just the right texture for making exquisite sushi.

Fresh, high-quality fish and other toppings and fillings are also essential to making great sushi. This book teaches you how to choose the best fish and other seafood for sushi and where to hold your knife to cut the meat for each presentation. You'll also learn which vegetable fillings and vegetarian toppings are perfect for making sushi and how to prepare them. Recipes are included for pickling, sautéing, steaming, and roasting ingredients to create intriguing sushi combinations, both traditional and contemporary, as well as for making classic accompaniments such as miso soup, pickled ginger, salads, and more.

The recipes in part 2 walk you through the preparation of the most popular types of sushi—*norimaki* (rolls wrapped in seaweed), *uramaki* (inside-out rolls), *temaki* (cone-shaped hand rolls), *nigiri* (hand-formed sushi), *gunkanmaki* (hand-formed sushi wrapped in seaweed), *temari* (rice balls), and *oshi* (pressed sushi). The book also includes recipes for *sashimi* (sliced raw fish), which is often served along with sushi at your favorite sushi bar, as well as classic sauces, sides, and salads.

In Japan, the art of sushi is steeped in tradition. At home, you can honor the spirit of these traditions without being bound by them. The goal is to make sushi that captures what you love about the cuisine while enjoying the freedom to break the rules so that the process is doable in your own kitchen.

ONE

Sushi Fundamentals

THE HISTORY AND CULTURE OF SUSHI

1

When Americans think of sushi, often it's fish that first comes to mind, particularly raw fish. But the word *sushi* actually means "vinegared rice." The name comes from the Japanese words *su*, meaning "vinegar," and *meshi*, meaning "rice." In Japan, sushi is defined as vinegared rice filled or topped with fish, shellfish, vegetables, or eggs—cooked, raw, or cured. Sushi has a long and storied history in Japan, dating at least as far back as the eighth century. Although historians disagree on just when sushi originated, everyone can agree that the cuisine has enjoyed centuries of popularity in Japan, where the preparation and presentation of the delicate, bite-size dishes has been honored for generations, but also modernized with the changing times and tastes. Today in Japan, sushi is both revered as an art and enjoyed as an everyday food.

A Brief History

The origin of sushi is not Japan but Southeast Asia, where fish was preserved in salt and lacto (lactobacillus)-fermented rice. The rice was simply a medium for storing and preserving the fish and was not eaten. The practice spread from Southeast Asia to Southern China and was probably introduced in Japan sometime in the eighth century. This form of sushi, called *nare-zushi* (fermented sushi), became an important source of protein, especially for Japanese Buddhists, many of whom abstained from meat.

In the earliest type of nare-zushi, called *funa-zushi*, prepared golden carp (*funa*) was layered with salted rice, weighted down, and left to ferment for anywhere from six to eighteen months. From the ninth to fourteenth centuries, only very wealthy Japanese could afford this delicacy. In fact, funa-zushi was considered so valuable that it was sent from outlying areas to the ancient capital city of Kyoto as a form of payment for taxes.

FIFTEENTH TO SEVENTEENTH CENTURIES

By the fifteenth century, Japanese cooks had discovered they could complete the fermentation process in as little as one month by adding heavier weights on top of the rice. The resulting fish was only partially pickled and so was aptly named *mama-nare-zushi*, or "raw" nare-zushi.

Just after the turn of the seventeenth century, the capital of Japan moved from Kyoto to Edo (now Tokyo), and a new merchant class was created, turning Edo into a bustling hub. Japan began ramping up food production, and both rice and products made from rice, such as rice vinegar, became commonplace. Instead of relying on the lengthy process of lacto-fermentation, Japanese cooks began adding vinegar to the rice, greatly reducing the time it took to make sushi. Still they continued to press the fish in a box with the vinegared rice and let it sit for a couple of hours, making the type of sushi known as *oshi-zushi*.

NINETEENTH CENTURY

It wasn't until the nineteenth century that this "instant" fermented rice began to be served with raw fish. By this time, Edo had taken its place as one of the largest, most densely populated cities in the world. Throughout the bustling city, sushi stalls popped up on busy street corners to serve oshi-zushi to hungry commuters in the evenings. Then, in the 1820s, a clever sushi-stand proprietor named Hanaya Yohei set up a stand on the Sumida River and got the bright idea to form the vinegared rice into a ball and top it with raw fish—and *nigiri-zushi*, or "finger sushi," was born.

The fish in this sushi was freshly caught from the nearby bay, so there was no need to ferment or preserve it. Using the quick rice preparation method of mixing cooked rice with seasoned vinegar and letting it sit for just a few minutes enabled Hanaya to quickly serve the throngs of customers who stopped by his stall on their way across the river. The people of Edo loved the quick-serve concept, and hand-formed sushi swept through the city and beyond. Other sushi makers soon began to follow suit, and nigiri, known as *Edomae* (Edo-style sushi), using ingredients local to Edo Bay, quickly became de rigueur.

TWENTIETH CENTURY

Over the next hundred years, the popularity of Edo's sushi carts blossomed. By the early 1920s, Edo had been renamed Tokyo, and sushi carts could be found all over the city. In 1923, the Great Kanto Earthquake, followed moments later by a 40-foot-high tsunami, obliterated Tokyo and drastically changed the course of history for Japan. An unexpected side effect of this tragedy was that property values plummeted drastically, and sushi stall operators were suddenly able to buy storefronts. Thirty years later, sushi, which until the earthquake had been almost exclusively a street food, was served almost exclusively in indoor restaurants, or *sushi-ya*. Improvements in refrigeration and the ability to ship fresh fish that came with the post-war economy completed sushi's transformation from a regional street food to a booming business. Sushi bars popped up across Japan and in other countries as well.

The first sushi restaurant in the United States opened in Los Angeles in 1966. Proprietors Noritoshi Kanai and Harry Wolff opened Kawafuku Restaurant, offering traditional hand-formed sushi, in LA's Little Tokyo. Japanese businessmen soon discovered the restaurant and brought their American colleagues there for what was then considered an exotic meal. A few years later, in 1970, a sushi bar opened in Hollywood, this one catering to the stars. Sushi rose to a whole new level of acceptance and popularity in America. Suddenly, sushi was cool. Today you'd be hard pressed to find a large American city that doesn't have at least a dozen sushi bars.

Tsukemono: The Fermented Foods of Japan

 *Tsukemono* are Japanese pickles—usually vegetables, but sometimes fruits or fish—often preserved in salt, brine, soy sauce, miso, sake lees (sediment), or fermented rice bran. These pickles are served alongside nearly every meal to balance the colors, flavors, and cooking methods required in traditional Japanese cuisine. Some of the most popular Japanese pickles are:

Asazuke: Thinly sliced Japanese cucumbers quickly pickled in a vinegar and sugar brine.

Gari: Young ginger sliced paper thin and marinated in a vinegar and sugar brine. Gari is often served with sushi as a palate cleanser.

Beni shoga: Red ginger pickled in *umeboshi* brine (made from ume plums).

Oshinko (or Takuan): *A crunchy pickled* daikon (Japanese radish) that takes on a bright yellow hue from the bacterium *Bacillus subtilis* during rice-bran fermentation and with the addition of persimmon peels, nasturtium flowers, or other colorings.

Shibazuke: Cucumbers and eggplant brined in salt and red shiso.

Umeboshi: Plums pickled in salt and red shiso.

Chef Jiro Ono

Known as the world's best sushi chef, Jiro Ono, who was born in the mid-1920s just as sushi was beginning to take off in Japan, has been honing his art since he was just nine years old. His restaurant, Sukiyabashi Jiro, which he operates with the help of his oldest son, holds the distinction of being the only sushi restaurant in the world to be awarded three Michelin stars. When President Obama visited Japan, this is where Prime Minister Shinzo Abe took him for dinner.

Contrary to what you might imagine, the restaurant is unassuming—ten seats tucked into a corner of a subway station in the basement of a Tokyo office building. Nonetheless, the restaurant and its proprietor were the subject of an episode of Anthony Bourdain's television show, *No Reservations*, and a popular documentary film, *Jiro Dreams of Sushi*. Chef Jiro and his restaurant have achieved mythic status.

Jiro's success is no doubt the product of his lifetime of experience, the quality of his ingredients, and the attention paid to every detail, no matter how small. Every morning, you'll find Jiro's son, Yoshikazu, at the Tsukiji fish market, where, guided by his father's teachings, he selects only the finest specimens. Jiro's techniques are those learned over more than 80 years of sushi making. His octopus is made tender through 45 minutes of massaging by hand (these days this job goes to an apprentice), his *nori* (seaweed) sheets are hand-toasted over a charcoal fire, his rice is kept exactly at body temperature, and each piece of sushi is hand formed by either Jiro or his son. You will not find a bottle of soy sauce or a dollop of wasabi at your place setting here. Because the chef seasons each bite to his exacting standards, nothing further is needed.

When you order the Chef's Recommended Special Menu at Sukiyabashi Jiro—after snagging a hard-to-get reservation weeks in advance—you can expect the meal to last about 20 minutes and cost nearly $300.

The Sushi Chef

In Japan, the role of a master sushi chef is revered. Whether a person starts as an apprentice at a sushi bar or by going to The Tokyo Sushi Academy—the only school in Japan devoted strictly to the art of making sushi—learning to make sushi properly is about much more than simply knowing how to form a rice ball and put a piece of raw fish on top.

THE APPRENTICE

Japanese sushi chefs typically train as apprentices for at least ten years before deemed ready to work behind the sushi bar. In the beginning, apprentices are stuck cleaning the kitchen and washing dishes. After a year or more, they are allowed to shadow their chef mentor, watching as the chef selects the day's fish from the market and—usually from several feet away—as the chef prepares the vinegared rice that is so crucial to properly made sushi. Eventually, the apprentice is permitted to stand next to the chef as the rice is prepared and wave a fan to cool it. Only after observing for a long period of time will the apprentice be trusted to make the rice, taught to cut the fish, and allowed to make sushi rolls at the side of the sushi bar. Finally, the trainee achieves master status and is allowed to stand behind the sushi bar and prepare the full range of sushi for customers—usually a decade or more after training began.

WOMEN BEHIND THE BAR

The role of sushi chef has traditionally been reserved for men. This is due at least in part to the fact that professional cooking has long been a male-dominated industry. But other "reasons" have been given to keep women from the profession. Among these are that women wear perfume, which can obscure the olfactory sense and therefore a woman's palate; that the job of a sushi chef is too physically demanding for women; that women's hands are too warm and will spoil the fish; and even that their monthly cycles could throw off their taste buds, rendering them incapable of making high-quality sushi.

Recent years have seen a noticeable shift in attitude, and more and more women, particularly in the United States but also in Japan, are becoming sushi chefs. In Japan, equal opportunity employment laws have only recently been passed, forcing sushi restaurants, along with other businesses, to hire and promote women. Another recent change in the Japanese employment law rescinded a ban on women working past 10 p.m. Thanks to these changes, the training doors to sushi bars have opened for women, even if they still have to fight against the tide of history to push their way through them.

A DAY IN THE LIFE

Once the apprentice—whether male or female—becomes a full-fledged master sushi chef, the real work begins. A sushi chef's day typically begins in the early morning hours, when the fish for the day's service is selected. Next the whole fish must be broken down, gutted, skinned, and sliced. Vegetables, pickles, and other garnishes are also prepared each day. And then the all-important rice must be made. First the rice is thoroughly rinsed, and then it is steamed until the grains are perfectly tender. It is then transferred to a large wooden bowl (*hangiri*) and tossed with vinegar that has been seasoned with sugar and salt. The rice is carefully folded with a wooden paddle (*shamoji*) to distribute the vinegar evenly and also cool the rice down.

By the time dinner service begins, all of the toppings, fillings, and garnishes have been prepped, the rice has been prepared, and the fish and shellfish have been readied for serving. The real fun begins as customers arrive and the sushi master shows off his or her skills with a sharp knife and nimble hands, forming firm but tender balls of rice topped with perfectly sliced fish, adding a stunning garnish, and serving customers with a flourish. From the time the restaurant opens until the last customer of the night leaves, the sushi chef is a performer on the stage that is the sushi bar.

Sushi Etiquette

Dinner in a sushi bar is different from a meal in a typical Western-style restaurant, especially if you sit at the sushi counter, where you'll order directly from the sushi chef. These are, in fact, the best seats in the house, since you get a front-row view of the fish ready to be sliced and served and of the chef creating sushi masterpieces. To further enrich your dining experience as well as pay homage to the chef, there are a few etiquette guidelines to keep in mind:

Upon Being Seated In a traditional sushi restaurant, as soon as you are seated—either at a table or at the sushi bar—you will be given a wet towel rolled up on a wooden dish. Unroll the towel and use it to gently clean your hands; then roll it back up and place it back on the wooden dish. Keep the rolled-up towel to the side of your plate, where you'll be able to wipe your fingers on the towel as needed throughout the meal.

Ordering If you are seated at the bar, you may order your sushi directly from the sushi chef, but do not ask him for drinks, water, extra napkins, or the check. Ask a waitperson for those items. Likewise, if you are seated at a table, order your sushi from your waitperson.

Preparing to Eat The little dipping bowl placed at your seat is for soy sauce. Pour no more than about a tablespoon of soy sauce into the dipping bowl. Wasabi should not be added to the soy sauce.

Sushi will usually be served with a small mound of wasabi paste on the side. This is meant for seasoning the fish. Note that the sushi chef will often add a swipe of wasabi between the rice and fish, so additional wasabi may be unnecessary. However, if you like your sushi with more of a kick, feel free to use your chopstick or a finger to add an additional smear of the paste to your fish.

When you dip your sushi into the soy sauce, dip it fish-side down; otherwise, the soy sauce will soak into the rice. Not only will you get too much soy sauce, but the nigiri will fall apart when you try to eat it.

If a piece of sushi comes pre-sauced, dipping it in soy sauce is unnecessary.

Eating It is totally acceptable to eat sushi with your fingers. Use the wet towel to wipe them between bites. Sashimi and foods other than sushi, however, should always be eaten with chopsticks.

Sushi is usually meant to be eaten in one bite because the sushi chef composes each piece to provide a perfect balance of flavor. Of course, sometimes the pieces are too big. In these cases, it is perfectly acceptable to eat it in two bites.

The pickled ginger served alongside sushi is meant as a palate cleanser, to be eaten between pieces of sushi.

Eating sushi is similar to tasting wine. You always want to start with the most delicate, mildest-flavored (halibut, snapper, sea bass, shrimp) fish first, moving on to richer fish (tuna, yellowtail, trout, scallops, oysters, clams), and finishing with the richest fish (tuna belly, sea urchin, salmon eggs). It's best to start with the simplest single-filling rolls and move on to those with more fillings. If you aren't sure where to begin, feel free to ask the sushi chef for advice.

The Mercury Issue

Fish and shellfish are a fantastic low-fat, low-calorie source of high-quality protein and other important nutrients, including heart-healthy omega-3 fatty acids, but some types contain potentially concerning levels of mercury. If you enjoy aquatic fare more often than the FDA-recommended 8 ounces (about 2 meals) per week—especially if you choose the types with high doses of mercury—the pollutant may build up in your tissue and cause problems. Pregnant women, nursing mothers, and young children in particular should limit the amount of mercury-containing fish in their diets.

Unfortunately, many of the most popular fish used in sushi tend to be high in mercury. If you are concerned about limiting mercury, tuna—including bluefin, yellowfin, bigeye, and albacore, as well as mackerel, sea bass, and yellowtail—should be eaten only in very limited quantities. Low-mercury fish and shellfish alternatives include salmon, snapper, eel, scallops, clams, crab, salmon roe, flying fish roe, squid, trout, octopus, abalone, sea urchin, and shrimp.

Is This Sushi Authentic?

 Since its first appearance in Japan centuries ago, sushi has been an evolving cuisine. Changing technology, economic conditions, and tastes have kept sushi chefs on their toes, constantly reinventing the art of sushi making while staying true to the important traditions. While it's true that a master Japanese sushi chef must train for many years to achieve his post behind the sushi bar, there are well-trained sushi chefs in other parts of the world who are equally obsessive about using fresh ingredients and delivering clean, balanced flavors. Whether making nigiri in Tokyo or maki in San Francisco, a good sushi chef uses only the best quality ingredients and puts them together in a deliberate and artful way. But sushi is always changing with the times and is heavily influenced by the location in which it is made.

In Japan

Nigiri remains the most popular form of sushi. Simple rolls may make appearances, but they are usually filled with one or two items: cucumbers or pickled radish, for instance. You'll see a wide variety of seafood used in sushi, but the best Japanese restaurants will serve only what is at the peak of freshness in the market that day, rather than the always-available, wide variety of flash-frozen seafood found on Western sushi bar menus. But lest you think Japanese people are entrenched in tradition, you'll find modern kaiten-zushi restaurants—serving sushi conveyor-belt style—are extremely popular throughout the country.

In Other Countries

Maki rolls are much more common throughout the world than they are in Japan. In fact, you'll find regional special rolls in the most unlikely places—from the Philadelphia roll that includes cream cheese and smoked salmon to Mexico's Tampico roll with fresh chilies, China's Peking roll filled with Peking duck, or Norway's herring roll.

Uramaki, or inside-out rolls, are an American invention, first introduced as the California roll in Los Angeles in the 1960s, when Americans had not yet discovered a taste for seaweed and preferred their rolls with just rice on the outside.

Ingredients, too, vary widely by location. For instance, although you'd never see avocado in sushi in Japan, it is a common ingredient in American sushi, again dating back to the 1960s in California when enterprising sushi chefs substituted it for tuna, its fattiness making it a good alternative, to appease customers who weren't keen on eating raw fish.

While these types of sushi may not be traditional, they are still authentic to an ever-evolving worldwide sushi cuisine.

After the Meal When paying your bill, leave the customary tip as you would in any full-service restaurant in the United States. Finally, thank your sushi chef. If you'd like to do so in Japanese, say, *"Domo arigato."*

Since most of the rules around eating sushi are meant to enhance the eating experience, they don't need to change when you are dining on sushi in your home, although you can be a bit more relaxed about following them. The most important rule to remember is to savor each and every bite and appreciate the flavors and textures offered by the different toppings and fillings.

Sushi Today

Today's sushi—both in Japan and around the world—is a far cry from its origins as carp preserved in lacto-fermented rice. The modern-day version is both a revered culinary art form that can cost you a pretty penny to enjoy in a high-end sushi restaurant and a quick, healthy fast-food item that you can grab ready-made and packed to go from just about any supermarket.

What began in Southeast Asia as a necessary, but rudimentary, way to preserve fish evolved over time, as it traveled east to Japan. The Japanese took sushi in and transformed it into something entirely new—a way of combining simple, everyday foods into works of art—from both a visual and culinary standpoint. The Japanese may not have invented sushi, but they imbued it with its artistic image by creating stunning arrangements and serving them in the quiet elegance you'll find in most fine sushi restaurants today.

THE WESTERN INFLUENCE

As the popularity of sushi grew, both in Japan and in other parts of the world, it evolved to incorporate ingredients available not just in Tokyo Bay (formerly Edo Bay) but also around the world. Westerners, it turned out, were squeamish about eating raw fish and seaweed. Invented in Los Angeles in the late 1960s, the California roll—an inside-out roll containing cooked crab, avocado, and cucumber with rice on the outside instead of a seaweed wrapper—proved the perfect stepping-stone sushi for the uninitiated. And it sparked a new trend toward "fusion sushi," which combined Japanese tradition with Western influences. Little by little, Westerners began to venture into the realms of raw seafood, and the sushi industry adapted to serve Western tastes.

The fact that sushi began its spread throughout the United States in the 1970s is no coincidence. At the time, newly health-conscious Americans were looking for foods lower in calories, fat, and cholesterol than the red meat–heavy fare they were used to. The combination of rice, fish, and vegetables, as well as the relative absence of heavy sauces or deep-fried foods, made sushi especially appealing. Fish is naturally low in calories and high in omega-3 fatty acids, giving

Chirashi-Zushi

 Chirashi means "scattered," which describes how this type of sushi is served—scattered over a bowl of sushi rice. There is no need to roll or shape anything, which makes this type of sushi especially quick and easy to prepare.

Chirashi hardly needs a recipe—and you won't find one in this book—since the idea is simply to compose a beautiful arrangement with a balance of flavors using the ingredients you have on hand. Simply fill a wide bowl with some sushi rice (enough for one person) and arrange your ingredients artfully on top, placing contrasting or complementary colors, shapes, and textures next to one another. Toppings can include anything from sashimi (tuna, halibut, yellowtail, eel, etc.) to pickled vegetables, seasoned mushrooms, sliced or shredded tofu or fresh vegetables (cucumbers, avocado, daikon), omelet, or sliced hard-boiled eggs, sliced fish cakes, tsukemono (Japanese pickles), or other items. Garnish with shredded omelet, strips of nori, radish sprouts, or sliced scallions. As with all sushi preparations, aim for a balance of color, flavor, and texture. Chapter 5 offers some great ideas for chirashi toppings.

it a positive effect on cholesterol levels. Other ingredients in sushi have health benefits as well. Rice is a low-fat source of carbohydrates and protein, ginger aids digestion and boosts the immune system, and wasabi is high in vitamin C, aids digestion, and possesses antibacterial and antiseptic qualities. It's no wonder that sushi took off as a cuisine in the United States during the health-conscious 1970s.

SELF-SERVE AT HALF THE PRICE

Meanwhile in Japan, forces were at work to transform sushi in its homeland. In 1958, a man named Yoshiaki Shiraishi watched beer bottles being carried through a factory on a conveyor belt and got a bright idea—conveyor belt sushi, or *kaiten-zushi.* Using the conveyor belt system, in which servings of sushi sit on a conveyor belt that runs past each seat, allowing customers to grab the dishes they want as they pass, would serve the dishes more efficiently, bringing down the cost. As Japan's economy took off in the 1980s, kaiten-zushi restaurants became extremely popular as family dining options. When Japan's economy collapsed in the early 1990s, Japanese people increasingly turned to inexpensive restaurants, and again, the kaiten-zushi establishments fit the bill.

ON EVERY CORNER OF THE WORLD

In Japan today, nigiri—a hand-formed ball of rice topped with a slice of raw fish—remains the most popular type of sushi, while here in the United

States, the fortuitous invention of the California roll paved the way for sushi's widespread acceptance and foreshadowed the long-standing popularity of Americanized *maki* rolls, filled with complicated combinations of ingredients.

The California roll may just be the most popular sushi in the United States today, and it's joined by a host of fanciful rolls, including the dragon roll (an inside-out roll usually filled with eel, cucumber, and tempura shrimp topped with avocado), rainbow roll (a California roll topped with tuna, yellowtail, salmon, shrimp, and avocado), spicy tuna roll (norimaki filled with minced raw tuna mixed with mayonnaise and hot sauce), dynamite roll (an inside-out roll with shrimp tempura, cucumber, flying fish roe, and spicy sauce), and the rock 'n roll (an inside-out roll filled with eel and avocado and coated with sesame seeds).

These days you'll find sushi in just about every corner of the world. It is haute cuisine for the moneyed elite, a healthy protein source for those who eschew red meat, or a quick midday meal for workers in downtown office buildings.

Sushi in Your Home

With all the history and tradition behind the cuisine, you may think sushi making is best left to the professionals. But the truth is that in Japan, sushi is often made by home cooks and served as a casual family meal. With the tips, advice, and recipes in this book, you can create that same casual family-meal experience in your own home.

This book guides you through the entire process of making sushi, with advice on what equipment to use, where to find ingredients, and how to select the freshest fish. You'll learn how to make perfect sushi rice, form balls, use seaweed as a wrapper, and garnish with style.

A master recipe is provided for each type of sushi—nigiri (hand-formed sushi), norimaki (rolls wrapped in seaweed), uramaki (inside-out rolls), *gunkanmaki* (battleship sushi), *temaki* (hand rolls), *temari* (rice balls), and *oshi* (pressed sushi). Each sushi preparation is thoroughly explained with step-by-step instructions for how to create it yourself. Also included in the book are recipes for all the accompaniments needed to serve a complete sushi meal, including soups, salads, sauces, and garnishes.

EQUIPMENT AND INGREDIENTS

2

Many of the culinary items needed to make sushi are the same ones used by home cooks throughout the Western world. But there are a few required pieces of equipment and food items that are not likely to be found in the typical American kitchen. Some ingredients also may not be available in your regular supermarket. This chapter details the materials you will need as well as where to get it all. With the right equipment and ingredients, great sushi is just a few rolls away.

Equipment

In any cooking endeavor, having the right tools at your disposal makes the job both easier and more fun. That's not to say that to enjoy making sushi, you have to go out and spend a small fortune on equipment. In fact, you probably own many of the necessary items: a strainer, measuring cups, cutting boards, mixing bowls, and a pot or even a rice cooker for cooking rice. Other needed items that are unique to sushi preparation can be found in a Japanese market or ordered online.

ESSENTIALS

Japanese fish knife or other sharp knife While you could use a good-quality, sharp chef's knife to make sushi, a Japanese knife is highly recommended. Japanese knives are specially designed for cutting raw fish and other tasks specific to sushi making. They are made of thin carbon steel, are sharper than stainless steel knives, and are sharpened only on one side, allowing them to slice through fish without damaging the cells.

A sushi chef will have a number of knives for specific tasks—a cleaver, a vegetable knife, a boning knife, and an all-purpose knife for slicing fish and meats, among others—but a home sushi maker can easily get away with one good chef's knife and a smaller paring knife. Choose knives that feel good in your hand and are well balanced: When you grip the knife by its handle, it shouldn't feel heavily weighted toward either the handle or the blade.

Keep your knives clean, washing them by hand, never in the dishwasher, and drying them immediately after washing. Store your knives in a knife block or in protective sleeves to prevent them from banging against other utensils in your drawer and becoming dull or chipped. Japanese knives should be sharpened only by hand using a whetstone rather than a steel knife sharpener or grinding blade, or better yet, take them to a professional knife sharpener as needed.

Flat bamboo or plastic rice paddle A bamboo rice paddle is ideal for folding your seasoned vinegar into your sushi rice and for scooping rice because its soft material won't crush or smash the grains of rice. Because bamboo is porous, rice won't stick to it, either. You can also use a plastic rice paddle (these are often included with electric rice cookers) in a pinch.

Bamboo sushi rolling mat Made of many thin bamboo sticks woven together into a flexible mat, this inexpensive tool is essential for making symmetrical, tightly wrapped maki. Look for the type with flat slats. There are two sizes of bamboo rolling mats. The standard larger maki sushi mat (usually about 10 inches square) is the one you'll need for the recipes in this book. When you are finished using the mat, wipe it clean, rinse with warm water, and dry thoroughly before storing.

NICE TO HAVE

Rice cooker While purists may argue that sushi rice needs to be cooked in a pot on the stove top, many sushi chefs now use rice cookers to cook their rice. You don't need to spend a lot of money to get a good rice cooker. A basic model, where you simply add rice and water and flip a switch, will do fine, though the top-of-the-line models offer features that will cook your rice to perfection by measuring the moisture content and adjusting the cooking time. If you are buying a rice cooker, choose one that cooks at least 8 cups of rice. Keep in mind, though, that you can use a regular saucepan with a tight-fitting lid to cook your rice on the stove top.

Know Your Knife

Japanese kitchen knives are made using the same techniques developed more than 1,000 years ago to make the samurai swords (*katana*) of legend. Like the exalted samurai swords, modern Japanese cooking knives are forged from carbon steel (often coated with a softer, more flexible steel with the harder carbon steel only exposed at the cutting edge) and characterized by their single, super-sharp edges. Just as the samurai depended on the quality of their swords, good-quality kitchen knives are the lifeblood of a modern-day sushi chef.

A sushi chef usually brings his own set of knives to work in the kitchen. Many chefs own two complete sets of knives, as a knife needs to rest for a day after sharpening to rid it of the metallic odor that may sully the flavor of the food cut with it. Having two sets of knives allows the chef to sharpen his knives every day.

The home sushi maker needs only one good, sharp, large knife. You can use a good-quality 6- or 8-inch chef's knife. A *santoku* knife— a Japanese all-purpose knife—is also an excellent choice. Santoku knives have very sharp blades featuring a dimpled pattern that causes sticky foods to release more easily, making them ideal for slicing raw fish. Most quality knife manufacturers offer both chef's knives and santoku knives. A few good brands to consider include Wüsthof, J. A. Henckels, Shun, and Misono.

In general, the more you spend on a knife, the better the quality. A more expensive knife will be constructed of higher-quality steel that will hold its edge longer and be constructed in such a way that, with proper care, it will last a lifetime.

Wooden rice bowl A wide, low-sided, unvarnished wooden rice bowl is ideal for mixing sushi rice, as the shape hastens the cooling process. Additionally, the porous wood absorbs excess moisture, which helps make the rice just the right texture. The wooden bowl should be soaked in water and wiped dry before using to keep the rice from sticking to the bowl. After using, wash it in cold water without dish soap and dry well. If you don't have a wooden rice bowl, use a large, wide, nonmetallic (plastic, glass, or ceramic) bowl to mix your sushi rice.

Electric fan Sushi rice must be cooled quickly in order to keep it from turning mushy or overly sticky. Traditionally, this has been accomplished

A Brief History of Chopsticks

 Billions of people around the world—virtually all cultures in East Asia including China, Japan, Korea, Vietnam, and Taiwan—have used chopsticks for centuries. They were invented in China as early as 1200 BC, when they were used as cooking utensils, great for plucking food from pots of steaming hot water or oil. Sometime around AD 500, when cooking resources were scarce, it became common to cut food into small pieces in order to cook it more quickly. Knives at the dinner table were no longer needed to cut food into bite-size pieces, and chopsticks proved useful tools for bringing the small morsels of food to one's mouth. One hundred years later, chopsticks began to appear at dinner tables throughout East Asia.

While the basic form was the same—two sticks manipulated with the fingers to handle food—styles diverged. In China, the tips were blunt, while in Japan, the chopsticks were usually made from a single piece of wood and connected at their base with pointed tips.

by fanning the hot rice with a handheld fan. An electric fan set on medium and aimed at the rice as you fold in the seasoned vinegar turns a once slightly arduous task into an easy one-person job. If you don't have an electric fan, don't worry. You can use a paper fan or even a stiff piece of cardboard as a handheld fan.

Oshi-zushi mold (*Oshibako*) If you plan to make pressed sushi (oshi-zushi), you might want to invest in a wooden or plastic mold made for the purpose. There are three pieces to the oshi-zushi mold: a box with vertical slits cut into the sides for slicing and two flat pieces used to press and compact the rice and toppings. If you don't have a sushi mold, you can use two square baking pans of the same size (such as 8-by-8-inch pans). Line one pan with aluminum foil, and then layer in your ingredients. Top with the second pan, and weight it down. Let it set for 30 minutes. Unmold the sushi, and then slice it with a sharp knife.

Cooking chopsticks Kitchen chopsticks are longer than the type used for eating, and they are often made of metal, as metal chopsticks are ideal for handling raw fish. It may not come naturally at first, but once you get used to using these in the kitchen, you will find them indispensable. The chopsticks can be used to stir sauces, beat eggs, lift and move small pieces of food in a hot pan, and arrange food on serving plates.

Chopsticks (for eating) Japanese chopsticks are made of wood and are usually about 8 inches long. They are used for eating everything from sashimi to rice and pickled vegetables. While it is acceptable to eat sushi with the hands, sashimi and other foods should always be eaten with chopsticks.

Fresh Ingredients

To make great sushi at home, you must first stock up on a range of Japanese ingredients. Short-grain rice, seaweed, wasabi, rice vinegar, and Japanese soy sauce are all crucial elements. Fortunately, with sushi's persistent popularity in the United States, these ingredients can often be found in your regular supermarket. If you are lucky enough to have a Japanese market in your area, all the better. They will have everything you need. If not, all the pantry staples you need can be easily ordered online.

For fresh products, quality is key. This means you may need to shop at various markets to acquire everything you need. Buy produce at a good produce market or farmers' market. Buy fish at a reputable fish shop, where you can be assured that the fish is fresh and of the highest quality.

FISH AND SEAFOOD

Anyone who has been to a sushi bar knows that the variety of fish and seafood available is dizzying. With so many choices, how does a newcomer to sushi making decide what to buy? Following are some of the most popular fish and seafood used for sushi.

Tuna

Several types of tuna are used for sushi, including bluefin (*maguro*) and yellowfin (*ahi*). *Toro* is the highly prized fatty tuna belly. Good tuna is a rich red color with a mild flavor and a pleasing melt-in-your-mouth quality. When buying tuna for sushi, look for fillets that are at least 1 inch thick with nice, even red coloring. Avoid tuna that has lots of visible white sinews in it, as these can be tough and fibrous. Buy tuna in fillets.

▸ *Tuna slicing tip:* Slice across the grain into pieces that are about 3 inches wide and ¼ inch thick for use in nigiri or sashimi.

Yellowtail

Yellowtail may refer to several different species of fish, but when used in sushi, it is usually Japanese amberjack. Often appearing as *hamachi* on menus, the Japanese word is more accurately used with farmed yellowtail. Light in color, yellowtail is an oily fish with a smooth texture and rich, buttery flavor. Yellowtail is usually sold in fillets.

► *Yellowtail slicing tip:* Slice across the grain into pieces that are about 3 inches wide and ¼ inch thick for use in nigiri or sashimi.

Salmon

Salmon is one exception to the "fresh is best" rule for sushi fish. Because it spends part of its life in fresh water, salmon is more likely to carry parasites than other sushi fish. There are three ways to rid salmon of parasites: smoking or curing, cooking, or freezing at a very low temperature. Fortunately, most of the salmon you'll find in US markets has been previously frozen, but check with your fishmonger to be sure. When choosing salmon for sushi, opt for fillets rather than steaks, as they will be easier to cut to the right shape.

► *Salmon slicing tip:* Slice across the grain into pieces that are about 3 inches wide and ¼ inch thick for use in nigiri or sashimi.

Snapper and Halibut

Snapper and halibut are delicate white fishes. When served very fresh, they have a mild, sweet

KNOW THIS FISH **Bluefin Tuna**

Bluefin tuna is the single most prized fish in the world today—a whole fish can sell for as much as $2 million. As if the price tag weren't shocking enough, as recently as 50 years ago, it was considered "garbage fish," caught for sport and used to make cat food.

Historically, Japanese diners eschewed the meaty, strongly flavored fish, preferring milder species to bluefin (and other tunas including yellowfin and bigeye). This may have been partly due to the fact that in the mid-1800s, tuna was plentiful in Japan. Cheap and readily available, it was considered, at best, a good filler protein. Budget-minded restaurateurs found that aging tuna for a few days mellowed its flavor. By slicing it thin and dousing it with soy sauce, they could disguise the strong taste of the fish even more, making it an ingredient that would fill patrons up while keeping a restaurant's costs down.

The sea change, so to speak, arrived in the 1970s, when Japanese consumers began to appreciate more strongly flavored meats, including beef and meaty tuna varieties. By this time, the bluefins' numbers had thinned significantly in Japanese waters, but the fish were plentiful off the Atlantic coast of the United States. US fisheries began shipping the fish to Japan for a tidy profit, and its image turned from a fish that "even a cat would disdain" to a delicacy as sought after as the truffles of Italy and France.

flavor and flesh that is quite delicate. Refrigerating fresh snapper or halibut for several hours reduces its moisture content, making it firmer and deepening its flavor. They are usually sold in fillets.

► *Snapper and halibut slicing tip:* Slice across the grain into pieces that are about 3 inches wide and ¼ inch thick for use in nigiri or sashimi.

Mackerel

An oily, strongly flavored fish, mackerel is known to spoil quickly. It can only be eaten raw as soon as it is caught. When it is served as sushi, it is usually salt-cured for several hours and rinsed with rice vinegar before serving (see Cured Mackerel Oshi, page 147). Mackerel is often sold whole, but it is challenging to fillet, so ask your fishmonger to do it for you.

► *Mackerel slicing tip:* Slice across the grain into pieces that are about 3 inches wide and ¼ inch thick for use in nigiri or sashimi.

Shrimp

Black tiger shrimp is fairly easy to find in the United States and is great for sushi, as it is similar in taste to the pricey karuma shrimp, which is considered the best to use for sushi in Japan. Shrimp is most commonly purchased frozen and served lightly cooked—poached or steamed—when used in sushi. Raw shrimp (*ama ebi*) is a delicacy, but it must be served very fresh, which can be difficult to find in the United States. Some good fishmongers or Asian markets sell live spot prawns, which are worth the price if you can find them.

► *Shrimp slicing tip:* How shrimp should be sliced will depend on what it is being prepared for. The recipes in this book that call for shrimp give specific preparation instructions.

Crab

Cooked crab, usually Alaskan king crab, is a key ingredient in California rolls. Depending on the season and where you live, you can buy live crabs and steam and crack them yourself, or you can buy crabs already steamed and cracked. Many fishmongers also sell crabmeat picked from the shell, but it is much more expensive than buying the whole crab and doing the work yourself. A large crab will yield about 25 percent of its full weight in meat (so a two-pound crab will yield about a half pound of crabmeat). If you can't find king crab, then blue crab or Dungeness can be substituted, though they won't be as meaty.

Many sushi makers use *surimi*, or crab sticks, an imitation crab made of processed white fish flesh shaped and colored to resemble snow crab or Japanese spider crab legs. Crab sticks are often used in place of real crab in California rolls, particularly the type you find packed to go in supermarkets.

► *Crab cracking and cleaning tip:* Wear gloves or use dishtowels to protect your hands when breaking the spiny legs of the king crab apart at the joints. Cut open the legs with kitchen shears or crack open with a nutcracker, and use a seafood fork to remove the meat.

Scallops & Clams

If you can get them, fresh scallops and clams are extremely sweet and make delicious toppings for nigiri.

Tsukiji Fish Market

Located in central Tokyo, between the Sumida River and the upscale Ginza shopping district, the famed Tsukiji Fish Market is the largest and busiest fish market on earth. The frenetic wholesale market opens in the wee hours, at 3:30 a.m., when fishermen bring in their products for auction and eager buyers come to place bids. Only a limited number of visitors are allowed in to witness the auctions, which wrap up by around 7:30 a.m. But the outer market, which is open to the public for retail sales, stays open until midafternoon. There you'll find more than 400 sea-based products, including everything from dime-a-dozen seaweed to precious caviar and tuna fresh from the sea. Everyone from chefs and resellers to housewives and tourists comes to buy cooking supplies—including fresh fish, vegetables, serving bowls, and fish knives—or to dine at one of the many seafood restaurants located there.

Live scallops are extremely difficult to come by, since scallops can't be kept alive long outside their natural environment. Most scallops are sold previously shucked and/or frozen, but opt for fresh if you can. Whatever you do, make sure you get your scallops from a trusted source. Many scallops are soaked in a phosphate solution that can give them an "off" flavor and make them watery. To avoid this, ask for "dry" or "dry-packed" scallops.

► *Clam cleaning tip:* Clams can and should be purchased live and shucked with an oyster shucker, but they can be gritty. To rid them of grit, place them in a large bowl with a tablespoon of salt and a couple tablespoons of cornmeal and cover with water. Refrigerate for 2 hours, and then rinse before shucking.

► *Scallop cleaning tip:* To shuck a live scallop, use an oyster shucker to pry it open a bit at the hinge. Then, with the flat side of the shell down, run a flexible fish knife across the inside of the bottom shell to separate the muscle from the shell, being careful not to cut into the flesh. Turn the scallop over so that the rounded side is down, and open the shell up completely. Using a spoon, scrape the muscle from the shell. Trim off the frill, stomach, and any other innards, leaving just the white meat. Using a paring knife, trim off the tough side-muscle piece. Rinse well.

Eel (*unagi*)

Eel is a flaky, richly flavored fish. It is never eaten raw and is considered difficult to cook.

For this reason, most eel fillets are purchased precooked and frozen. You can find eel in the freezer at any Japanese market, where it is usually sold in 8-ounce and 16-ounce packages. The fish can be defrosted overnight in the refrigerator or by placing the unopened package in a bowl for 30 minutes. Once sliced, heat the pieces under a broiler and brush with the sweet-savory soy-based sauce known as Eel Sauce (*Unagi Tare*) (page 59), which you can purchase in bottles at Japanese markets.

► *Eel slicing tip:* The fillets need only be sliced into nigiri-size pieces (about 3 inches wide and ¼ inch thick).

Fish roe (*ikura, tobiko, masago*)

The most common types of roe for sushi are salmon (*ikura*), flying fish (*tobiko*), and capelin (*masago*). Salmon roe is the largest of the three—pearl-sized, bright orange balls that burst and release a salty brine when you bite into them. Flying fish roe are small, orange, crunchy, and salty. They are often used as a garnish on uramaki (inside-out rolls) or added to other sushi dishes, but they can also be enjoyed on their own in preparations like gunkanmaki (battleship sushi). Capelin roe are even smaller than flying fish roe and do not naturally possess the same bright hue (food coloring is often added to brighten them). They do not have quite the same crunch and are considered a poor-man's substitute for flying fish roe. All three types of roe can be purchased at Japanese markets.

CHOOSING AND ORDERING FISH AND SEAFOOD

Selecting fish for sushi is one of the most intimidating aspects of home sushi making. Where do you buy it? How can you tell if it's fresh? What does "sushi grade" mean? These are all excellent questions, and knowing the answers can make the difference between delighting or disappointing your guests.

Making the Grade

First let's get the issue of "sushi grade" out of the way. To put it bluntly, the phrase "sushi grade" is meaningless. There are no governmental regulations or even guidelines as to what can be given this label. A fish seller can call any fish he likes sushi grade, but that doesn't mean you'd necessarily want to eat it raw.

Get to Know Your Fishmonger

In order to find fish that is, in fact, suitable for serving raw in sushi, find a good fish shop. You want to buy your fish in an establishment where you can talk to the fishmonger and ask questions about where the fish came from, how long ago it arrived in their shop, and if it has been frozen. Start by telling him or her that you are planning to use the fish for sushi and ask for the freshest fish. The monger may offer recommendations beyond the usual tuna and salmon, including local fish that are often very fresh and delicious.

Look Your Fish in the Eye

When seeking out fresh fish, it is best if the market has the whole fish so that you can see the skin. It should have shiny scales, moist and slippery skin, and eyes that are clear and bright. Most important of all, whether buying a whole fish or precut fillets, the flesh should be evenly colored, moist, firm, and resilient.

Though fresh fish is best, you don't have to rule out frozen fish. In fact, by law, any fish served raw in a restaurant in the United States is supposed to first be frozen for a period of time at a very low temperature to kill parasites (flash frozen). Still, you want fish that was frozen soon after it came out of the water (ideally on the boat) and that has not been frozen for long. It should have good, even color and firm, resilient flesh. A good fishmonger will be able to tell you if a previously frozen fish is suitable for sushi.

A Little Fish Goes a Long Way

When making sushi, you will want to have a variety of toppings and fillings, but be careful, as it is easy to buy far too much fish. Since the fish will be served with rice and other accompaniments, 4 ounces of fish and seafood per person should be plenty. For a dinner for four people, 1 pound of fish and seafood should be good. So, for example, you might buy 4 ounces of tuna, 4 ounces of salmon, 4 ounces of crab, and 8 scallops or clams.

Produce and Proteins

Being creative with sushi isn't only about fish and seafood, of course. The real fun is in combining those ingredients with vegetables and other food items. By using a variety of fish and other ingredients, you can create stunning displays that artfully balance color, flavor, and texture.

The most common vegetables used in sushi are those that are found in Japan:

Daikon radish is a large, white, strongly flavored radish that can be pickled or served raw, shredded, or cut into decorative shapes.

Radish sprouts are similar to the more familiar alfalfa sprouts but are sturdier and have a bright, peppery flavor that pairs well with many rich fishes and other sushi fillings.

Lotus root is the root of the water lily. It is crunchy and white and reveals a pretty honeycomb pattern of holes when sliced. It is usually cooked in water seasoned with sugar, rice vinegar, and soy sauce until it becomes soft but still retains a pleasant crunch. You can sometimes find lotus root fresh in Japanese markets, but you're more likely to see it frozen or pickled in vinegar.

Cucumber is frequently used in sushi to provide a contrasting cool and refreshing crunch to rich fishes and other ingredients. The long, slender Japanese cucumbers, which have fewer and smaller seeds, are ideal for sushi making, but you can substitute English cucumber if necessary.

Avocado is an American addition to sushi, but its pretty green color and smooth, rich mouth feel make it a welcome interloper. The fruit is also used in the popular dragon roll (see recipe, page 95) to create the skin of the dragon on the outside of the inside-out roll.

Scallions, also called green onions, are often thinly sliced and added to maki rolls to offer a visual contrast and a sharp flavor note to cut the richness of certain fish like salmon or yellowtail. They are also often used as a colorful garnish.

Tofu is a great vegetarian substitute for fish in sushi. It is often seasoned with soy sauce and/or rice vinegar and other seasonings and baked or sautéed before serving. Soft or silken tofu or firm tofu is best for sushi. *Inari-zushi* is a type of sushi in which vinegared rice and other ingredients are stuffed into a pouch made from deep-fried tofu (*abura age*). You can buy abura age in cans at Japanese markets.

Pantry Staples

Certain pantry staples are required for making great sushi, but thanks to the cuisine's popularity, many of these can be found in any large supermarket. If you have a Japanese market in your town, they will surely have everything you need. Otherwise, the Internet will provide. Marukai eStore is an online Japanese market that carries everything you could possibly need. Amazon.com also sells many of the necessary pantry items.

DRY GOODS

Rice Choose Japanese-style, short-grain rice for making sushi. Its high starch content gives it the right stickiness for making sushi rice. Traditionally, only white rice is used for sushi, but short-grain brown rice can be used as well. Look for rice labeled "short grain" or "sushi rice." Do not substitute medium- or long-grain rice, as they will not produce a sticky enough finished product to hold together.

KNOW THIS VEGETABLE
Japanese Cucumber

Japanese cucumbers tend to be narrower than the regular hothouse or English cucumbers you're likely to find in supermarkets in the United States. Usually 8 or 9 inches long and about 1½ inches in diameter, Japanese cucumbers are ideal for use in sushi because they have thin, delicate skin and very few seeds. They are also firmer as well as less watery and bitter than American or English cucumber varieties.

Japanese cucumbers are usually salted before slicing for sushi to soften the skin, giving it just the right texture for maki. To salt, rinse the cucumber in cold water and, without drying it, sprinkle the cucumber all over with about ¼ teaspoon of salt. Roll the cucumber around on a cutting board, and then rinse the salt off, dry the cucumber, and slice it as desired.

Nori These dried seaweed sheets—made of algae that has been washed and spread to dry in thin sheets—are used to wrap norimaki, gunkanmaki, and temaki. They are also sometimes used as garnish. Look for nori sheets that are dark green or black and tightly grained. Nori for making norimaki are usually almost square shaped—8 by 7 inches. Smaller nori (4 by 7 inches) are perfect for making temaki (hand rolls).

KNOW THIS CONDIMENT
Pickled Ginger

 Pickled ginger (*gari*) is tender-fleshed young ginger that has been very thinly sliced and marinated in a brine of vinegar and sugar. Gari is thought to be an essential accompaniment to sushi, but it is not meant to be eaten in the same bite. Instead, gari is eaten as a palate cleanser between bites of sushi. It is acceptable, however, to dip a piece of ginger into your soy sauce and use it as a brush to lightly season a piece of nigiri.

Gari made with very young ginger will have a natural pale pink hue, but most of the pickled ginger you find in markets and sushi restaurants has been colored with red or pink food coloring. You can buy natural pickled ginger without colorings. It will usually be a pale golden color.

Dried gourd (*kampyo*) Sold as long, thin strips, this traditional vegetable is delicious reconstituted in broth, diced, and added to sushi rolls or used as a garnish.

Dried shiitake mushrooms Dried shiitake mushrooms can be found at Japanese markets and many supermarkets. Before using, reconstitute them in warm water. They are a lovely addition to norimaki or temaki and are often included in vegetarian futomaki.

Bonito flakes Dried bonito fish flakes are used to flavor *dashi* (Japanese broth). They are sold in single-serving packets in Japanese markets. The flakes are added to hot water, along with other seasonings, to make stock.

Dried kelp (*kombu*) Dried kelp is used to flavor rice and dashi. The flavoring can be purchased in Japanese markets, health food markets, or online. It is an optional ingredient in sushi rice.

BOTTLED GOODS

In addition to dried goods such as bonito flakes, seaweed sheets, and rice, several bottled goods are used in sushi making. Again, many of these can be found in any large supermarket, and all can be found in Japanese markets or online.

Wasabi paste While fresh wasabi (Japanese horseradish) is ideal for sushi, it is hard to come by in the United States. Instead, you can use either a canned powdered wasabi that can be mixed with water to form a paste or you can buy ready-to-use paste in tubes. Many wasabi pastes are made with garden-variety horseradish and green food coloring, so be sure to read the ingredients label and buy one made with real wasabi if possible.

Soy sauce Soy sauce, made from soy beans fermented with wheat and salt, is an important seasoning in any type of Japanese cooking. Any soy sauce will do, but if you can, buy Japanese soy sauce, which is aged longer than Chinese soy sauce. Be sure to keep the bottle in the refrigerator after opening.

Rice vinegar Mildly flavored rice vinegar is essential for making proper sushi rice. Rice vinegar is also used to season and pickle vegetables and in salad dressings and other sauces. Buy the unseasoned variety so that you can control the amount of seasoning.

Miso Miso, a paste made from fermented soybean, is an important staple of Japanese cuisine. Cooked with dashi, it forms the basis of miso soup. Miso is also used to add depth of flavor and umami to sauces and salad dressings and as a seasoning for meat, fish, and vegetables. Miso's color ranges from pale golden to reddish-brown to very dark brown to black. Lighter misos tend to be milder in flavor and darker misos more intense. The most common misos are *shiromiso* (white miso), *akamiso* (red miso), and *awasemiso* (mixed miso).

Pickled ginger (gari) Very thinly sliced pieces of ginger are pickled in a mixture of rice vinegar and sugar. Pickled ginger is simple to make at home (see recipe, page 53), but it is also readily available in the refrigerated section of Japanese markets.

Sake Sake is a Japanese rice wine served as a beverage, and it is a perfect match for sushi or sashimi. Although much of the sake in the United States is sold heated, Japan produces many fine sakes that are best enjoyed at room temperature or lightly chilled. Sake is also used as a seasoning in cooking, especially in meat and fish dishes. If you don't have sake, you can substitute a dry sherry.

Mirin Mirin is a Japanese cooking wine made from fermented sticky rice. It is sweeter than sake or white wine, but any of these can be substituted in a pinch for another, as can dry sherry.

Eel sauce (unagi tare) Eel sauce is a glaze made of soy sauce, sugar, and sake. It is most commonly used with unagi (eel) for either sushi or *unagidon* (a rice bowl topped with cooked unagi), but it can be used to season other meat, fish, or vegetable dishes as well.

SUSHI RICE

3

To make sushi, one first has to make perfectly cooked and seasoned rice. This chapter details everything you need to know to make perfect vinegared rice for sushi, from selecting the type of rice to use to cooking, seasoning, and cooling it. ▣ While a sushi chef apprentice may train for years before he is even allowed to attempt making rice, any home chef can follow the simple instructions needed to make a good sushi rice that is both well seasoned and has a good texture for holding together in nigiri or maki. Follow these tips, and you will surely be successful.

Before You Make the Rice

Practice makes perfect. This doesn't mean taking on the life of an apprentice sushi chef and practicing for years to learn how vigorously to wash the rice before cooking. Just know that you may need to make sushi rice a few times before achieving the results you desire. You will soon discover that if the rice in your pantry is old, it will likely require a touch more water, or that you may prefer a seasoning mix with more salt or less sugar.

Choose carefully. The importance of choosing the right type of rice cannot be overstated. Traditional sushi rice is made with Japanese-style, short-grain white rice (*japonica* rice). This rice has just the right shape and starch content to hold together in balls for nigiri and for other forms of sushi. Brown rice can be used for sushi, but again, it must be short-grain brown rice. Sushi rice can be found at many large supermarkets, at a Japanese market, or online. Never choose long-grain or basmati rice when making sushi, as these simply won't work.

Follow the rules. There are certain tried and true rules for making sushi rice, and following them is key to success. These rules are discussed in detail later in this chapter. In a nutshell, the rules include: rinsing the rice well before cooking to rid it of excess starch, dissolving the salt and sugar fully in the vinegar before adding it to the rice, adding the seasoned vinegar mixture to the rice while it is still warm so that the grains fully absorb the seasoning, gently folding rather than stirring the vinegar into the rice to avoid breaking or crushing the rice grains, and keeping the rice at room temperature until ready to use.

Gather Your Materials

You need only a few tools and ingredients to make sushi rice. If you don't already have one, a rice paddle can be purchased at most cookware stores or Asian markets, but most of the materials are probably already in your kitchen cupboards and pantry.

EQUIPMENT

2-quart saucepan with a tight-fitting lid or an electric rice cooker (Instructions for cooking rice either on the stove top or in a rice cooker are provided in this chapter.)

Fine-mesh strainer or colander for washing and draining the rice

Shallow, wide bowl (Ideally, this is a wooden sushi rice bowl that has been soaked in water for 30 minutes. If you do not have a wooden sushi rice bowl, a wide glass, plastic, or ceramic mixing bowl is fine.)

Wood or plastic rice paddle

Electric or handheld fan or a small piece of stiff cardboard

Clean dish towel for covering the bowl of cooked rice

How to Make SUSHI RICE

The basis of any good sushi is perfectly cooked, delicately seasoned rice. Making the rice begins with rinsing the grains thoroughly and finishes with folding the vinegar into the cooked rice as it cools. The end result should hold together when formed into a ball, yet not be overly sticky or gummy. Each step is simple to follow, but it's by following each one perfectly that you will achieve the perfect sushi rice. This recipe is for white sushi rice. To make brown sushi rice, see the note at the end of this recipe.

1⅓ cups Japanese-style short-grain rice
1½ cups water
1 piece kombu, about 2 by 3 inches (optional)
3 tablespoons unseasoned rice vinegar
2 tablespoons sugar
½ teaspoon salt

1. In a large pot or bowl, cover the rice with cold water. Agitate the rice gently in a circular motion with your hand, swirling 4 or 5 times, and then drain the rice through a fine-mesh strainer. Return the rice to the pot or bowl, and repeat the process at least 3 or 4 more times, until the rinse water is mostly clear. Drain the rice a final time, and let it sit in the strainer for 30 minutes.

2. **Stove-top cooking method:** In a covered medium saucepan over medium heat, bring the drained rice and the water along with the kombu (if using) to a boil over medium heat. Continue to boil the rice for 4 minutes; then reduce the heat to low and let simmer for 10 minutes more. Do not lift the lid at any time while cooking the rice. At the end of 10 minutes, turn off the heat, but do not remove the lid. Let the rice stand in the covered pot for another 10 minutes. Discard the kombu (if using) before using the rice.

    Rice cooker method: If using an electric rice cooker, put the drained rice, water, and kombu in the rice cooker and turn it on. When the cooker indicates that the rice is done, turn the appliance off, without opening the cooker, and let the rice stand for 10 minutes. Discard the kombu (if using) before using the rice.

3. While the rice is cooking, prepare the sea-soned vinegar mixture. In a small saucepan over medium heat, combine the vinegar, sugar, and salt, stirring constantly. Do not let the mixture come to a boil, reducing the heat if needed. Continue cooking and stirring until the sugar and salt completely dissolve, about 3 minutes. Remove from the heat.

4. Transfer the rice to a large, wide shallow bowl. Using your rice paddle, spread the rice into an even layer across the bottom and sides of the bowl. If you are using an electric fan, set it a foot or two away on medium speed and aim it at the bowl; otherwise, have the hand fan or cardboard ready to use.

5. Immediately pour the seasoned vinegar mixture over the hot rice. Using your rice paddle, fold the rice over itself to mix in the vinegar. Do not stir the rice. Instead use a folding motion, spreading the mixture out across the bottom of the bowl every once in a while. Continue folding, fanning the rice by hand every so often if you are not using an electric fan, until the vinegar mixture is evenly distributed and the rice has cooled to room temperature.

6. Place a damp kitchen towel over the rice to keep it from drying out until you are ready to use it. Sushi rice can be kept this way for up to 12 hours. Do not refrigerate the rice before using or the texture will be ruined.

How to Make
BROWN RICE SUSHI

Brown rice is not commonly used in Japan, but it is possible to use it to make sushi rice. Brown rice is less starchy than white rice, so the finished result will not be as sticky as with white sushi rice. For this reason, brown rice is best used in norimaki rolls, which have seaweed on the outside to hold the rice together. As with white sushi rice, it is essential to use a short-grain variety of brown rice.

1⅓ cups short-grain brown rice

2 cups water

1 piece kombu, about 2 by 3 inches (optional)

3 tablespoons unseasoned rice vinegar

2 tablespoons sugar

½ teaspoon salt

1. Follow step 1 of the Sushi Rice Master Recipe (page 39) to rinse the brown rice.

2. **Stove-top cooking method:** In a medium saucepan over medium heat, bring the drained rice and the water along with the kombu (if using) to a boil. Cover, reduce the heat to low, and simmer the rice for 40 minutes more. Do not lift the lid at any time while cooking the rice. At the end of 40 minutes, turn off the heat, but do not remove the lid. Let the rice stand in the covered pot for another 10 minutes. Discard the kombu (if using) before using the rice.

   Rice cooker method: Read the instructions on your rice cooker, especially if you have only been using it to cook white rice, as some rice cookers have a brown rice setting. As with cooking white sushi rice, put the drained rice, water, and kombu (if using) in the rice cooker and turn it on (using the brown rice setting if the appliance has one). When the cooker indicates that the rice is done, turn the appliance off, without opening the cooker, and let the rice stand for 10 minutes. Discard the kombu (if using) before using the rice.

3. Follow steps 3 through 6 of the Sushi Rice Master Recipe (page 39) to season and cool the rice.

What Success Looks, Feels, and Tastes Like

The sushi you make can be only as good as the rice you prepare. This is why it is so important to rinse, cook, and season the rice according to strict guidelines and using the exact proportions—at least until you've got the hang of making it. Read all the instructions, and have all the equipment at hand before making the rice. Above all, be patient with yourself as you become familiar with each step of the process. Perfect sushi rice balances many seemingly contradictory conditions. It should be sticky enough so that it holds together well, but not so sticky that the rice is gluey or gummy. It should be tender, but not overly soft or mushy. It should be flavorful, but not too sweet (sugar), tart (vinegar), or salty.

Troubleshooting Guide

Making sushi rice can be somewhat challenging the first few times. There are a number of places where the process can go astray and leave you with a less than stellar result. Following are a few of the common mishaps, with advice for preventing them.

The problem: Mushy rice

The reason: Mushy rice can be the result of too much water used in cooking.

How to avoid it: Be sure to drain the washed rice very well before transferring it to the cooking pot or rice cooker. Carefully measure the water used for cooking the rice, using a liquid measuring cup (ideally one with a pour spout with gradations on the side of the cup) as opposed to a dry measuring cup, which is meant to be filled to the top with dry ingredients and leveled off. Rice can also become mushy if it is left to sit in the pot for too long after cooking. Set your timer for 10 minutes once the active cooking has finished and the heat has been turned off, and remove the lid as soon as the timer goes off. Another reason for mushy rice is that it was not thoroughly cooled before it was covered with a towel. The rice should be at room temperature before being covered.

The problem: Undercooked rice

The reasons: There are a number of errors that can lead to undercooked rice. If your rice is not tender enough, it could mean that it was simply not cooked for long enough. Another possibility is that you didn't use enough water. Again, water should be measured using a liquid measuring cup, while rice should be measured with a dry measuring cup to ensure that you have the proper amounts of each. Cooking rice on the stove top in a pot with an ill-fitting lid can also lead to undercooked rice because too much steam escapes during cooking.

How to avoid it: If steam escapes from your pot during cooking, try covering the pot with aluminum foil before putting the lid on top. Likewise, if the heat is too high during stove top cooking, the liquid will evaporate too quickly, leaving you with rice that is not tender. Be sure to reduce the heat to the lowest possible setting for the last 10 minutes of cooking time.

The problem: Inconsistently cooked rice

The reason: You have probably put too much rice in your pot or rice cooker.

How to avoid it: If cooking rice on the stove top, be sure to use a saucepan big enough so that the rice or water doesn't spill over the top as it cooks. Also make sure that the lid fits tightly. Double-check that you are using the correct amounts of rice and water given in the Sushi Rice Master Recipe (page 39). If using an electric rice cooker, carefully follow the guidelines in the instructions provided with your electric rice cooker to make sure you're not trying to cook too much rice for the size of rice cooker you have.

The problem: Lumpy rice

The reason: You waited too long to add the vinegar mixture to the rice. The vinegar mixture should be added to the rice before it cools down so that it can be fully dispersed and absorbed by the rice.

How to avoid it: To avoid rice that holds together in clumps, be sure to add the vinegar mixture while the rice is still hot and to fold the vinegar into the rice quickly, but gently, until the vinegar is thoroughly incorporated and the rice has cooled to room temperature.

The problem: Overly sticky rice

The reason: If your rice comes out too sticky or starchy, it could mean that it wasn't rinsed thoroughly enough.

How to avoid it: Rinse the rice several times, agitating it gently with your hand, until the water is nearly clear.

TWO

Sushi Recipes

Once you've purchased high-quality fish for your sushi or sashimi, prepared the non-seafood sushi fillings and condiments, and made the rice, it's time to get out your knife and get down to business. Fish should be kept chilled, so prepare your work area before removing the fish from the refrigerator. ⊡ Before cutting, rinse the fish gently under cold water and pat it dry with paper towels. Using needle-nose pliers, remove any bones. To cut, place the handle of the knife where you wish to begin slicing, and pull the knife blade back through the fish in one pass. Wetting the knife with a damp paper towel between cuts will keep the fish from sticking to the blade.

SLICING FISH
For Maki

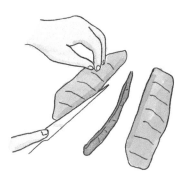

1 Cut the fillet lengthwise, across the grain, into three sections: the narrow, brown or red middle section known as the bloodline and the two usable sections on either side of it. Discard the bloodline.

2 To remove the skin, lay one piece of the fish on the cutting board, skin-side down, parallel to your body. Hold it down with the palm of your hand. Starting with the side closest to you, insert the tip of a boning knife between the skin and flesh, and make a shallow cut to separate the two.

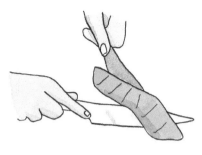

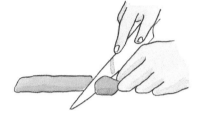

3 Use your fingers to hold the exposed flap of skin while sliding a large, sharp knife into the gap. Tilt the blade down slightly and facing away from you. Slice from right to left (or left to right, depending on which hand holds the knife) to separate the skin from the flesh, lowering the knife so that it is almost parallel with the cutting board as it moves across the fish. Discard the skin. Repeat with the other piece of fish.

5 Cut each slice into ½-inch-wide sticks. For spicy rolls, dice or mince the strips into whatever size pieces you prefer.

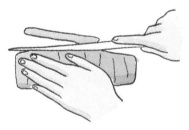

4 Place one piece of the fillet on the cutting board parallel to your body. Using a large, sharp knife, position the handle of the blade on the far side of the fish. The blade should be roughly perpendicular to the grain of the flesh. Slide the blade toward you along the length of the fillet to cut ½-inch-wide slices. Repeat with the other piece of fish.

SLICING FISH
For Sashimi, Temari, Nigiri, Gunkanmaki, and Oshi

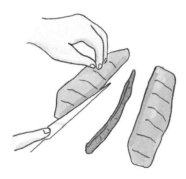

1 Cut the fillet lengthwise, across the grain, into three sections: the narrow, brown middle section where the grain changes directions, known as the bloodline, and the two usable sections on either side of the bloodline. Discard the bloodline.

2 Cut off the area at the bottom of the belly on both pieces of fish where the grain changes direction again to end up with a rectangular block of fish.

3 To remove the skin, lay one piece of the fish on the cutting board, skin-side down, parallel to your body. Hold it down with the palm of your hand. Starting with the side closest to you, insert the tip of a boning knife between the skin and flesh, and make a shallow cut to separate the two.

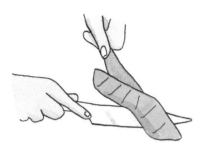

4 Use your fingers to hold the exposed flap of skin while sliding a large, sharp knife into the gap. Tilt the blade down slightly and facing away from you. Slice from right to left (or left to right, depending on which hand holds the knife) to separate the skin from the flesh, lowering the knife so that it is almost parallel with the cutting board as it moves across the fish. Discard the skin. Repeat with the other piece of fish.

6 To cut the fish straight up and down for sashimi, place the handle of the blade on the far edge of the fish, and cut by pulling the knife straight down and toward yourself in one smooth stroke. For temari, nigiri, gunkanmaki, and oshi, you may want to cut the fish at a 45-degree angle. Use the same cutting technique, but start with the knife at a 45-degree angle to the fish. Cut slices anywhere from half an inch thick for sashimi to paper thin.

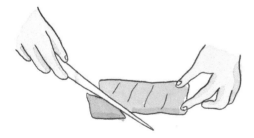

5 Hold the knife perpendicular to the grain of the fillet, with the cutting edge at one corner of the rectangle. Slide the blade toward you across the fillet to cut a triangle, so that the end of the fillet is at a diagonal to the sides. Reserve the triangle to use in norimaki.

7 Reserve all the odd-shaped bits of fish for use in norimaki or minced fillings, such as spicy rolls.

BASICS

4

The art of sushi lies in combining many elements of flavor, texture, and color to create cohesive bites that delight the senses. Of course, good sushi relies on perfect sushi rice, as detailed in the previous chapter. Fresh fish that has been delicately cut is also an important element. But what really makes sushi shine is an assortment of bright and flavorful accompaniments, from rich relish to spicy sauces. By preparing a handful of these basic recipes, you can take your sushi from simple to simply exquisite. ▢ This chapter offers recipes for the basic elements of good sushi, including Pickled Ginger (page 53) and Toasted Nori (page 52). It also offers several recipes for accompaniments and sauces that will take your sushi to the next level, like the most popular sauces and a basic Stock (page 55) that can be used for seasoning a variety of dishes.

Toasted Nori

YIELD VARIES | PREP TIME: NONE | COOK TIME: 5 MINUTES

Nori is the edible, dried, and pressed seaweed used to wrap certain types of sushi. Toasting nori deepens its flavor and improves its texture for use in sushi. While much of the nori you'll find in the market is already toasted, toasting it again will still improve your results. Nori can be toasted either on a gas stove top or under the broiler. Directions for both methods follow.

Nori sheets

To toast nori over a gas burner

1. Turn the burner to medium-high.

2. Using chopsticks, tongs, or your fingers (be careful not to burn yourself!), hold a single nori sheet by the edge and place it a few inches above the flame. Move the sheet side to side two or three times, and then flip it over to toast the other side. Toast the nori very lightly, without blackening or blistering the dried seaweed. Repeat until you have toasted as many nori sheets as you will need.

To toast nori under the broiler

1. Preheat the broiler.

2. Place the nori sheets in a single layer on a baking sheet, and toast under the broiler for about 30 seconds. Remove the baking sheet, flip the nori sheets over, and toast for another 20 seconds. Be sure to toast the nori very lightly, without blackening or blistering it.

Pickled Ginger GARI

MAKES ABOUT ¾ CUP | PREP TIME: 10 MINUTES, PLUS OVERNIGHT TO MARINATE | COOK TIME: 3 MINUTES

Pickled ginger accompanies every serving of sushi. It is meant to cleanse the palate between bites. Good-quality pickled ginger is available for purchase, but it is also easy to make at home. To get the trademark pink color naturally, use very young ginger. Older ginger is fine to use, but the color will be more beige. To cut the ginger paper thin, use a mandoline or vegetable peeler.

1 (6-inch) fresh ginger piece, peeled and cut into
   paper thin slices

½ cup sugar

½ cup water

½ cup unseasoned rice vinegar

1 teaspoon salt

1. Put the sliced ginger in a clean jar or nonreactive (glass or ceramic) bowl.

2. In a small saucepan over medium heat, mix together the sugar, water, vinegar, and salt, stirring frequently, until the sugar and salt are completely dissolved, about 3 minutes.

3. Pour the hot vinegar mixture over the ginger. Let the ginger cool for several minutes, then cover and refrigerate overnight. Pickled ginger can be kept for up to a month, refrigerated.

Chile-Daikon Relish

MAKES ABOUT 1 CUP | PREP TIME: 10 MINUTES

This spicy relish is quick to make and adds a welcome punch to hand rolls and other dishes. Add a spoonful to a dish of Ponzu Dipping Sauce (page 61) to create a spicy citrus-soy dipping sauce. You can use any type of red chile you like, or substitute a teaspoon or two of chili paste or a smaller amount of cayenne.

1 daikon radish (about 8 ounces), peeled
1 small red chile, finely minced

1. In a medium bowl of cold water, soak the daikon for about 5 minutes.
2. In a separate medium bowl, grate the daikon.
3. Add the chile and mix well. Serve immediately.

Stock DASHI

MAKES ABOUT ½ QUART | PREP TIME: 5 MINUTES | COOK TIME: 5 MINUTES

Dashi is a Japanese stock used to season many Japanese dishes, including omelets (known as dashimaki tamago) and mushrooms for which there are recipes in this book. Dashi is usually made from bonito flakes (thinly shaved flakes of dried, smoked tuna) and kombu (dried kelp). To make vegetarian dashi, double the amount of kombu and omit the bonito flakes.

2 cups water, divided
2 (2-by-3-inch) kombu pieces
¾ ounce bonito flakes

1. In a large saucepan over medium heat, combine the water and kombu and bring just to a boil. Remove the kombu, and add the bonito flakes without stirring.

2. As soon as the mixture returns to a boil, remove the stock from the heat and let it sit for about 2 minutes, until the bonito flakes settle to the bottom of the pot.

3. Strain the dashi through a fine-meshed sieve. Cool the stock to room temperature, and store in a covered container in the refrigerator for up to 3 days. Dashi can be frozen for up to 3 months.

Omelet DASHIMAKI TAMAGO

SERVES 4 | PREP TIME: 10 MINUTES, PLUS 10 MINUTES TO COOL | COOK TIME: 10 MINUTES

Tamago is a thick Japanese rolled omelet that is often sliced and used as a topping for nigiri or a filling for maki. Dashimaki tamago is tamago seasoned with dashi, sugar, and sake or mirin. It is moist, slightly sweet, and full of flavor. A bamboo sushi-rolling mat is optional, but using one helps shape the roll.

6 eggs
½ cup Stock (page 55)
2 tablespoons sugar
1 tablespoon sake or mirin
1 tablespoon neutral-flavored oil such as grapeseed or safflower

1. In a medium bowl, beat the eggs with chopsticks or a fork (the idea is to mix the eggs without incorporating too much air, so don't use a whisk.) Add the stock, sugar, and sake, and beat to combine well.

2. In a medium omelet pan, add the oil, using a paper towel to spread the oil evenly. Reserve the oil-soaked paper towel.

3. Heat the oiled pan over medium heat. When the pan is hot, spoon one-quarter of the egg mixture into the pan so that it coats the entire bottom. As the egg cooks, pop any bubbles that form with chopsticks or a fork.

4. When the bottom of the egg is set, but the top is still a bit runny, use a spatula to fold one quarter of the omelet toward the center; then repeat on the opposite side to create two straight sides on the right and left.

5. Next, beginning with the rounded side closest to you, roll the omelet over itself, about 2 inches at a time, toward the far side of the pan.

6. If needed, use the oil-soaked paper towel to add additional oil to the pan. Spoon one-third of the remaining egg mixture into the pan so that it covers the entire bottom of the pan (it will run under and around the already cooked portion of egg).

7. Repeat steps 3 through 6 above until you have used up all the egg mixture.

8. If using a bamboo sushi-rolling mat, transfer the omelet to the mat and gently roll it up. If not using a mat, transfer the omelet to a cutting board and cover with a towel. Let cool for 10 minutes.

9. Unwrap or uncover the omelet, and slice into ¼-inch-thick slabs.

Cooking tip: A square Japanese omelet *(tamagoyaki)* pan is ideal for giving the tamago its familiar rectangular shape, but this recipe gives instructions for using a round skillet. If you happen to have a tamagoyaki pan, by all means use it. You won't need to fold the sides of the omelet in before rolling, but otherwise the procedure remains the same.

Seasoned Mushrooms

SERVES 4 | PREP TIME: 5 MINUTES | COOK TIME: 20 MINUTES

Simmered in dashi and seasoned with soy sauce, sugar, and mirin, these mushrooms are delicious as a side dish or garnish and also make a nice addition to maki. If you can't find fresh shiitake mushrooms, the same amount of dried shiitakes can be substituted. Rehydrate the dried mushrooms by soaking them in warm water for 20 minutes before adding them to the broth.

1¼ cups Stock (page 55)
2 tablespoons mirin
2 tablespoons sugar
2 tablespoons soy sauce
8 fresh shiitake mushrooms, stemmed and
    sliced into strips

1. In a medium saucepan, stir together the Dashi, mirin, sugar, and soy sauce. Add the mushrooms and bring to a boil over medium heat. Reduce the heat to medium-low, and let the mixture simmer until the liquid is mostly evaporated, about 15 minutes.

2. Drain the mushrooms. Slice the mushrooms. Let them cool to room temperature if using for sushi, or serve them warm as a side dish.

Eel Sauce UNAGI TARE

MAKES ABOUT ¾ CUP | PREP TIME: 2 MINUTES | COOK TIME: 45 MINUTES

Eel sauce is a thick, sweet-savory glaze that is usually brushed over eel (unagi) when it is served with rice or in sushi. Made by simmering soy sauce with rice wine and sugar, it is almost like a Japanese-style barbecue sauce. It can also be used on other types of sushi, including vegetarian sushi.

½ cup mirin
3 tablespoons sake
5 tablespoons sugar
½ cup soy sauce

1. In a small saucepan over medium heat, mix together the mirin and sake and bring to a boil. Stir in the sugar and cook, continuing to stir until the sugar is completely dissolved, about 2 minutes.

2. Reduce the heat to low, add the soy sauce, and simmer, stirring occasionally, until the sauce thickens, about 30 to 40 minutes. Remove the sauce from the heat and let cool.

3. The sauce will continue to thicken as it cools. If the sauce becomes too thick, reheat, stirring in a bit of sake or water. Eel sauce can be stored in a covered container in the refrigerator for up to 2 weeks. Be sure to warm the sauce before using.

BASICS

Spicy Mayo

MAKES ABOUT ¼ CUP | PREP TIME: 2 MINUTES

Spicy mayo is what gives spicy tuna rolls their kick. The mayo is also a fantastic all-around condiment any time you want to add a little something to vegetable, meat, or even fruit dishes. Drizzle it over sashimi, temaki, nigiri, or maki. When choosing a mayonnaise base for this recipe, many Japanese food lovers swear by Kewpie mayonnaise from Japan. Thanks to the addition of monosodium glutamate (MSG), Kewpie is sweeter and has a more rounded flavor than the American dressing, but your regular mayonnaise will work just fine here. This recipe is easily halved or doubled.

¼ cup mayonnaise
1 tablespoon sriracha sauce
1 teaspoon Asian sesame oil

In a small bowl, stir together the mayonnaise, sriracha sauce, and sesame oil. Serve immediately.

Ponzu Dipping Sauce

MAKES ABOUT 1 CUP | PREP TIME: 2 MINUTES

Ponzu is a citrus-flavored soy sauce. It is often used as a dipping sauce or as a sauce for cooked fish, but it can also be brushed onto raw fish for sushi. Bottled yuzu juice can be found in Japanese markets.

½ cup soy sauce
¼ cup unseasoned rice vinegar
¼ cup lemon or yuzu juice

In a small bowl, stir together the soy sauce, rice vinegar, and yuzu juice. Use immediately or store, covered, in the refrigerator for up to a month.

Lemon-Wasabi Sauce

MAKES ABOUT 3 TABLESPOONS | PREP TIME: 2 MINUTES

This sauce is so simple—made with just two ingredients—but it packs such a bright burst of flavor, you'd never know it. Use Lemon-Wasabi as a dipping sauce for Cured Mackerel Oshi (page 147) or drizzle it over nigiri or maki when you want a bit of citrus and spice.

Juice of 1 lemon
1 teaspoon wasabi paste

In a small bowl, stir together the lemon juice and wasabi paste until well combined. Use immediately.

Made from fermented rice, sake is often referred to as Japanese rice wine. The many types of sake can make ordering the alcoholic beverage bewildering. Sake falls into six basic types, each requiring different methods of brewing and rice polished (milled) to different degrees. Each type has distinct flavor characteristics.

Junmai-shu, considered "table sake," is the lowest grade of sake with no specifications for how finely the rice should be milled. Junmai-shu is not fortified, meaning no distilled alcohol is added. Junmai-shu sakes are full bodied and more acidic than other sakes. This type of sake is often served warm.

   Honjozu or *Junmai-honjozu* are considered "premium" sake. They are made with lightly milled rice (30 percent polished away). Honjozu is fortified with a touch of distilled alcohol, giving it a lighter, smoother flavor than junmai-honjozu. The flavor profile of junmai-honjozu is similar to that of junmai-shu. This type of sake is usually served at room temperature.

   Ginjo or *junmai-gingo* are "super premium" sake, made with rice 40 percent polished away. Ginjo has been fortified with distilled alcohol. Both ginjo sakes are light, fragrant, and complex. They are best served slightly chilled.

   Daiginjo or *junmai-daiginjo* have the highest sake grade, requiring rice that was milled by at least 50 percent. Daiginjo has been fortified with distilled alcohol. Both daiginjo sakes are full bodied and complex and are best served chilled.

   Namazake is unpasteurized or "fresh" sake. These sakes have fresh, bright, fruity flavor, similar to that of a young wine. Because they are unpasteurized, they must be kept cold.

   Nigori is unfiltered sake. Instead of being clear like other sakes, nigoris are cloudy white. Their flavor is rich and slightly sweet.

SASHIMI

5 Sashimi refers to any sliced meat served raw with condiments or garnishes—the word comes from *sa* meaning "knife" and *shi* meaning "fillet." Unlike with sushi, the meat is neither rolled into nor placed on top of sushi rice. Sashimi is usually made with fish or seafood, but it can also be made with other meats, such as beef or venison. The slices are arranged artfully, usually with a garnish of shredded daikon or shiso leaves. ▣ Sashimi and sushi are very often served together, which is why a chapter on how to make sashimi is included in this book. In Japan, sashimi tends to be served before the sushi and enjoyed with a glass of sake. ▣ Because sashimi is not combined with seasoned sushi rice, vegetables, or sauces, the quality of the fish is especially important. High-quality tuna, sea bream, mackerel, yellowtail, and shellfish, including scallops, prawns, and octopus, are the most popular for sashimi.

Tuna Sashimi
with Sesame Seeds and Scallions

SERVES 4 AS AN APPETIZER OR PART OF A MULTICOURSE MEAL | PREP TIME: 10 MINUTES | COOK TIME: 1 MINUTE

This simple dish is the very essence of sashimi— just very fresh fish, sliced in generous slabs and garnished with a sprinkling of crunchy toasted sesame seeds and zesty sliced scallions. You can use any type of fresh tuna for this dish or substitute salmon if you prefer. Serve with soy sauce and wasabi paste for dipping.

2 teaspoons white sesame seeds
8 ounces tuna fillet
½ cup shredded daikon
1 scallion, thinly sliced

1. In a small skillet over medium-high heat, toast the sesame seeds, shaking the pan frequently until the seeds become fragrant and begin to pop, about 1 minute. Transfer the seeds to a small dish.

2. Following the "Slicing Fish" instructions for sashimi on page 48, slice the fish into ¼-inch slices.

3. Divide the daikon evenly among 4 serving plates, placing it in a pile in the middle of each plate. Divide the fish evenly among the plates, leaning the slices up against the daikon.

4. Sprinkle each serving with a quarter of the toasted sesame seeds, and arrange a quarter of the scallion slices on top of each. Serve immediately.

Troubleshooting tip: If the fish feels too soft to slice cleanly, try chilling it in the freezer for 20 minutes or so before slicing.

Marinated Mackerel Sashimi SHIME SABA

SERVES 4 AS AN APPETIZER | PREP TIME: 10 MINUTES, PLUS 24 HOURS TO MARINATE

Mackerel has a storied history in Japan—and even a historic road named after it. The Mackerel Highway brought seafood to landlocked Kyoto in the days before refrigeration. With no way to keep the fish cold, it had to be preserved in order to survive the journey to the capital city. Preserving mackerel by lightly curing it in salt and then pickling the fish in rice vinegar remains popular today. In fact, many say a restaurant's shime saba is a good measure of the skill of its chef.

2 mackerel fillets, about 4 ounces each, skinned

1 tablespoon plus 1 teaspoon salt, divided

1½ cups unseasoned rice vinegar

1½ tablespoons sugar

1 tablespoon mirin

1 small Japanese cucumber

Soy sauce, for serving

1. Sprinkle the fillets on each side using the 1 tablespoon of salt. In a glass baking dish or other nonreactive dish wide enough to hold the fish in a single layer, place the fillets. Cover and let sit for 30 minutes.

2. Rinse the fillets gently under cold water to remove the salt. Pat dry and set aside. Drain any liquid that has accumulated in the baking dish.

3. In the drained baking dish, combine the vinegar, sugar, mirin, and the remaining 1 teaspoon of salt. Stir until the sugar is dissolved. Place the fish in a single layer in the dish. Cover and refrigerate for at least 24 hours.

4. Cut the ends off of the cucumber, and then slice a small piece off one side to create a flat edge. Cut the cucumber into 3-inch pieces. Working with one piece at a time, cut the cucumber into very thin, flat, 3-inch-long slices. Stack the slices and cut into matchstick pieces.

continued ►

5. Just before serving, remove the fish from the baking dish, letting the vinegar solution drain from the fillets, and pat dry. Following the "Slicing Fish" instructions for sashimi on page 48, slice the fish very thinly.

6. Divide the cucumber among 4 small serving plates, placing the matchstick pieces to the side of each plate. Divide the fish evenly among the plates, leaning them up against the cucumber garnish. Serve immediately with soy sauce for dipping.

Troubleshooting tip: Mackerel tends to have quite a few small bones. Use needle-nose pliers to remove the bones before curing.

Salmon Sashimi with Ginger and Chili Oil

SERVES 4 AS AN APPETIZER | PREP TIME: 15 MINUTES | COOK TIME: 3 MINUTES

Salmon is a rich, fatty, and very flavorful fish. The zingy ginger, pungent chili oil, and bright cilantro add an exciting bite. Drizzling the hot oil over the fish just before serving warms it just enough to bring out all of the flavors.

1½ teaspoons sesame seeds

¼ cup low-sodium soy sauce

2 teaspoons freshly squeezed lime juice

2 teaspoons orange juice

8 ounces salmon fillet

1¼-inch fresh ginger piece, cut into
    thin matchsticks

1 tablespoon snipped chives

2 tablespoons neutral-flavored oil such as
    grapeseed or safflower

1 teaspoon Asian sesame-chili oil

¼ cup cilantro leaves

1. In a small skillet over medium-high heat, toast the sesame seeds, shaking the pan frequently until the seeds become fragrant and begin to pop, about 1 minute. Transfer the seeds to a small dish.

2. In a small bowl, mix the soy sauce with the lime juice and orange juice.

3. Following the "Slicing Fish" instructions for sashimi on page 48, slice the fish into ⅛-inch slices. Divide the slices of fish evenly among 4 serving plates, arranging them decoratively. Sprinkle the ginger and chives over the fish. Drizzle the soy sauce mixture over the tops of the fish.

4. In a small saucepan over medium-high heat, add the neutral-flavored oil and sesame-chili oil and heat until very hot, about 2 minutes. Using a spoon, drizzle the oil over the fish. Sprinkle with the toasted sesame seeds and cilantro leaves. Serve immediately.

Troubleshooting tip: When planning to serve salmon raw, be sure to buy fish that has been flash frozen when caught, as this kills any potential parasites.

Scallop Sashimi with Seasoned Mushrooms

SERVES 4 AS AN APPETIZER | PREP TIME: 10 MINUTES

Delicate sea scallops, which have a sweet, clean flavor, pair beautifully with earthy shiitake mushrooms. If you've made the mushrooms ahead of time, this dish only takes as long to make as it does to shuck the scallops.

12 sea scallops
Seasoned Mushrooms (page 58), sliced thin
2 tablespoons wasabi paste
Soy sauce, for serving

1. Rinse the scallops gently in cold water, then butterfly them by slicing almost all the way through the narrow side of the flesh with a thin, sharp knife.

2. Divide the mushrooms evenly among 4 small serving plates, and arrange the scallops, open like a book, on top of each. Place a dollop of wasabi paste on the side of each plate. Serve immediately, with soy sauce for dipping.

Troubleshooting tip: To ensure that your scallops are very fresh, buy them live and still in their shells. You can pop the shells open with a thin, sharp knife or an oyster shucker. Slide the knife under the scallops to cut the muscles that attach them to the shells. Remove any fringe and orange parts, so that only the white muscle remains.

Snapper Sashimi with Chives and Curry Oil

SERVES 4 AS AN APPETIZER | PREP TIME: 5 MINUTES, PLUS 60 MINUTES TO STAND

Snapper is a mild white fish with a firm bite that makes it ideal for sashimi. The hot, curry-infused oil in this recipe warms the fish just a touch, bringing together the intense flavors of the curry and fresh ginger with the mild sweetness of the fish.

FOR THE CURRY OIL

1 tablespoon curry powder

Pinch salt

Water, as needed

¼ cup neutral-flavored oil such as grapeseed or safflower

FOR THE SASHIMI

8 ounces snapper fillet

¼ cup snipped chives

1½ teaspoons finely minced ginger

To make the curry oil

In a small mixing bowl, mix the curry powder and salt with enough water to make a paste. Slowly stir in the oil. Let the paste stand 60 minutes before using.

To make the sashimi

1. Slice the fish into about ¼-inch-thick slices following the instructions for "Slicing Fish" for sashimi on page 48.

2. Divide the slices evenly, arranging them on 4 small serving plates. Sprinkle the chives over the top of each.

3. In a small saucepan over medium-high heat, add the curry oil using a spoon, leaving behind the paste at the bottom of the bowl. When the oil is very hot, add the ginger and remove from the heat immediately. Spoon the hot oil over the fish, and serve immediately.

Troubleshooting tip: If you can't find super fresh snapper, substitute with yellowtail, halibut, or fluke.

MAKI ROLLED SUSHI

6

Maki means "roll" in Japanese and refers to any type of filled, rolled sushi including norimaki (rolls with nori on the outside), uramaki (rolls with rice on the outside), and temaki (cone-shaped hand rolls). Maki make for a great introduction to preparing sushi at home because they are easier to make than *nigiri* and generate a large amount of sushi relatively quickly. From the sushi bar to your kitchen table, it's no wonder maki are the most popular type of sushi in the West.

How to Make NORIMAKI

Norimaki are rolled sushi filled with rice and fish or vegetable fillings and wrapped with nori. The tightly wrapped rolls are sliced into bite-size rounds for serving. Thin rolls, known as hoso-maki, generally contain just one or two ingredients. A half sheet of nori should be used for rolling them. Medium-sized and thick rolls, known respectively as chumaki and futomaki, require rolling with a full-sized sheet of nori. The individual recipes in this chapter will note whether to roll with a half sheet or full-size sheet of nori.

INGREDIENTS

4 (8-by-7-inch) Toasted Nori sheets (see page 52)
2 cups Sushi Rice (page 39)
Fillings (fish sliced according to the instructions
    for "Slicing Fish" for maki on page 46, sliced
    vegetables, eggs, tofu, or a combination)
2 cups water mixed with 2 tablespoons rice vinegar,
    for wetting hands

EQUIPMENT

Bamboo sushi-rolling mat
Sharp knife

1 Prepare your work area by setting out your Toasted Nori sheets, Sushi Rice, fillings, toppings, and garnishes, as well as the bowl of vinegared water.

2 Lay the sushi-rolling mat on your work surface with the flat sides of the slats facing up.

3 If you are making maki with one or two ingredients, fold each nori sheet in half, and then cut along the break using a knife or kitchen scissors to yield 4 sheets (4 by 7 inches each). If you are making maki with two or more ingredients, use a full-sized sheet of nori.

4 Lay one ½ sheet or full sheet of nori on the mat, shiny-side down, with one of the long sides facing you. Line up the sheet on the edge of the bamboo mat.

5 Moisten your hands in the bowl of vinegared water; then, using your wet hands, scoop up about ½ cup of rice and press it onto the nori in an even layer about ¼-inch thick. Using your fingertips, gently distribute the rice without smashing the grains. The rice should cover the nori all the way to the short edges and to just one of the long edges.

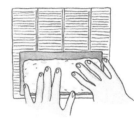

For thin rolls: Leave about a ¾-inch strip of the nori without any rice on it along the long side farthest from you.

For medium-size rolls: Leave about a 2-inch strip of the nori without any rice on it along the long side farthest from you.

For thick rolls: Leave about a 1-inch strip of the nori without any rice on it along the long side farthest from you.

continued ▶

6 Lay one quarter of the fillings in a 1½-inch-wide strip along the long edge closest to you.

7 Lift the mat at the filled edge, and gently roll it away from you until the mat touches the rice. Press down gently to shape the roll; then repeat the process until the roll reaches the unfilled edge of the nori. Run a wet finger along the unfilled strip of nori, and press the nori onto the roll to seal the edge. Using the mat, form the roll into a tight cylinder. Repeat with the remaining ingredients to form 4 rolls.

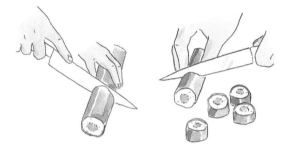

8 To slice each roll into rounds, begin by cutting each roll in half. Moisten the blade of a sharp knife with water. Position the handle end of the blade crosswise at the center of the roll and draw the knife toward you, all the way to the point, slicing through the roll in one smooth move. Repeat with the remaining 3 rolls.

9 Cut each half roll in half again using the same cutting method. Next cut each quarter roll in half so that you have 8 rounds for each roll.

10 Serve immediately. Storing Norimaki is not recommended, because the nori becomes soggy and the rice will become hard if refrigerated.

Tuna Roll TEKKA MAKI

SERVES 4 | PREP TIME: 15 MINUTES

Tekka maki has only one filling in addition to the rice and is considered hosomaki or "thin roll." This is the original style of maki—a simple, single-filling roll that is about 1½ inches in diameter. Using only one filling makes rolling easy, so it is a great starter roll if you are just learning to make sushi.

2 (8-by-7-inch) Toasted Nori sheets (page 52), cut in half to make 4 (4-by-7-inch) sheets
2 cups Sushi Rice (page 39)
1 teaspoon wasabi paste (optional)
4 ounces tuna fillet, cut into 4 strips about 1 inch wide

1. Follow the steps for How to Make Norimaki on page 74.

2. After following the direction to spread the rice on the nori, add a smear of wasabi paste (if using) down the center of the rice for each roll.

3. When directed to lay the filling, place one quarter of the tuna strips in a row along the long edge closest to you for each roll.

4. Proceed with rolling and slicing the rolls. Serve immediately.

Salmon and Scallion Roll SAKE NEGIMAKI

SERVES 4 | PREP TIME: 20 MINUTES

Rich salmon is complemented by the bright flavor of fresh scallion. This is a simple roll that combines two fillings inside the sushi rice while still remaining small and easy to handle. Feel free to substitute yellowtail for the salmon if you like.

2 (8-by-7-inch) Toasted Nori sheets (page 52), cut in half to make 4 (4-by-7-inch) sheets

2 cups Sushi Rice (page 39)

4 ounces salmon fillet, cut into 4 strips about 1½ inches wide

2 scallions, cut into thin strips about 2 inches long

1. Follow the steps for How to Make Norimaki on page 74.

2. When directed to lay the filling, place one quarter of the salmon and the scallion in a row along the long edge closest to you for each roll.

3. Proceed with rolling and slicing the rolls. Serve immediately.

Spicy Tuna Roll

SERVES 4 | PREP TIME: 20 MINUTES

The spicy tuna roll is one of the most popular types of sushi in American sushi bars. The raw tuna filling is mixed with a spicy mayonnaise, which gets its kick from sriracha hot sauce. This is a great way to use up all the odd-shaped bits you trim off a tuna fillet when slicing it for sashimi or nigiri.

4 ounces tuna fillet, diced or minced

2 tablespoons Spicy Mayo (page 60)

2 (8-by-7-inch) Toasted Nori sheets (page 52), cut in half to make 4 (4-by-7-inch) sheets

2 cups Sushi Rice (page 39)

1. In a small bowl, gently toss together the tuna and Spicy Mayo to mix well.

2. Follow the steps for How to Make Norimaki on page 74.

3. When directed to lay the filling, place one quarter of the tuna mixture in a row along the long edge closest to you for each roll.

4. Proceed with rolling and slicing the rolls. Serve immediately.

Rock 'n Roll

SERVES 4 | PREP TIME: 20 MINUTES | COOK TIME: 2 MINUTES

Cooked freshwater eel (unagi) is a popular sushi filling. The meat is rich and succulent, and it is almost always prepared with the thick, sweet-savory glaze known as Eel Sauce (page 59). You can buy cooked, frozen eel in any Japanese market. Defrost it in the refrigerator overnight or by placing the unopened package in a bowl of cold water for 30 minutes or so.

1 cooked eel fillet (thawed if frozen), about
     6 ounces, cut into strips
4 (8-by-7-inch) Toasted Nori sheets (page 52)
2 cups Sushi Rice (page 39)
¼ cup warm Eel Sauce (page 59), plus additional
     for serving
1 medium avocado, sliced into strips

1. Preheat the broiler.

2. On a baking sheet, place the eel in a single layer and broil for about 2 minutes, until the top begins to bubble a bit.

3. Follow the steps for How to Make Norimaki on page 74.

4. When directed to lay the filling, for each roll, place one quarter of the eel on the rice in a row along the long edge closest to you and brush with about a tablespoon of the sauce; then add a strip of avocado next to that.

5. Proceed with rolling and slicing the rolls, and serve immediately, drizzled with additional sauce if desired.

Shrimp, Asparagus, and Cucumber Roll with Flying Fish Roe

SERVES 4 | PREP TIME: 20 MINUTES | COOK TIME: 3 MINUTES

Poached shrimp is a great sushi filling for those who aren't quite ready for raw fish. The delicate, sweet flavor pairs especially well with earthy asparagus. Skewering the shrimp before poaching keeps them flat so that they are easy to use in sushi. You'll need 8 bamboo skewers.

8 medium shrimp, heads removed and deveined (see Cooking tip, page 82)

4 fat spears or 8 thin spears asparagus, trimmed

4 (8-by-7-inch) Toasted Nori sheets (page 52)

2 cups Sushi Rice (page 39)

1 small Japanese cucumber, cut into spears

2 tablespoons flying fish roe (tobiko)

1. In a large saucepan or stockpot (wide enough to hold the skewers) over medium-high heat, add enough water to cover the shrimp, lightly salt, and bring to a boil.

2. Meanwhile, insert a bamboo skewer through each shrimp from the head end straight through to the tail. This will keep the shrimp flat as it cooks. Place the skewered shrimp in the boiling water, and cook for about 2 minutes, until the shrimp is pink and opaque. Remove the shrimp from the water and let them cool.

3. Once the shrimp is cool enough to handle, remove the shells. Using a sharp knife, butterfly the shrimp by cutting along the inner curve, being careful not to cut all the way through the flesh.

4. In a medium saucepan over medium-high heat, add enough water to cover the asparagus. Lightly salt and bring to a boil. Meanwhile, in a medium bowl, add enough water and ice to cover the cooked asparagus. When the water in the saucepan is boiling, add the asparagus and cook for 1 minute.

continued ▶

Shrimp, Asparagus, and Cucumber Roll with Flying Fish Roe *continued*

5. Using tongs or a slotted spoon, transfer the asparagus to the ice water bath and let chill for a few minutes. Remove the asparagus, pat dry, and set aside.

6. Follow the steps for How to Make Norimaki on page 74.

7. When directed to lay the filling, for each roll, place one quarter of the shrimp (opened and flat), asparagus, and cucumber in adjacent strips on the rice running lengthwise and parallel with the long end of the sheet, and then sprinkle the roe over the top.

8. Proceed with rolling and slicing the rolls. Serve immediately.

Cooking tip: To devein shrimp with the shell still on, stick the sharp end of a skewer or toothpick into the back of the shrimp, about ¼ inch from the tail, between the first and second shell segments. Hook the point of the skewer under the dark vein (the intestinal tract), and slowly pull it out.

Scallop, Salmon Roe, and Cucumber Roll

SERVES 4 | PREP TIME: 20 MINUTES

Delicate and sweet, scallops make a delicious maki filling. Paired with salty salmon roe and crisp cucumbers, they are nearly irresistible.

4 (8-by-7-inch) Toasted Nori sheets (page 52)

2 cups Sushi Rice (page 39)

4 ounces scallops, halved or quartered if large

¼ cup salmon roe

1 small Japanese cucumber, cut into spears

1. Follow the steps for How to Make Norimaki on page 74.

2. When directed to lay the filling, for each roll, place one quarter of the scallops, salmon roe, and cucumber spears in adjacent strips on the rice running lengthwise and parallel with the long end of the sheet.

3. Proceed with rolling and slicing the rolls. Serve immediately.

Shrimp Futomaki

SERVES 4 | PREP TIME: 20 MINUTES

Futomaki means "big roll." This sushi typically contains five fillings, making a roll that is usually about 2½ inches in diameter. Rolling futomaki tightly enough that it holds together can be challenging, but once you've mastered the technique, the result is delightful—so many flavors, textures, and colors in one roll. Pickled daikon is a bright yellow, mild, pickled Japanese radish. It can be purchased at a Japanese market. You'll need eight bamboo skewers to prepare the shrimp.

8 medium shrimp, heads removed and deveined (see Cooking tip, page 82)

4 (8-by-7-inch) Toasted Nori sheets (page 52)

2 cups Sushi Rice (page 39)

4 long strips pickled daikon

Seasoned Mushrooms (page 58)

4 (7-by-1-inch) strips of omelet (page 56)

½ cup blanched spinach

1. In a saucepan or stockpot (wide enough to hold the skewers) over medium-high heat, add enough water to cover the shrimp. Lightly salt the water and bring to a boil.

2. Meanwhile, insert a bamboo skewer through each shrimp from the head end straight through to the tail. This will keep the shrimp flat as it cooks. Place the skewered shrimp in the boiling water and cook for about 2 minutes, until the shrimp is pink and opaque.

3. Remove the shrimp from the water and let cool. Once the shrimp is cool enough to handle, remove the shells. Using a sharp knife, butterfly the shrimp by cutting along the inner curve, being careful not to cut all the way through the flesh.

4. Follow the steps for How to Make Norimaki on page 74.

5. When directed to lay the filling, for each roll, place one quarter of the shrimp, daikon, mushrooms, omelet, and spinach in adjacent strips in that order on the rice running lengthwise and parallel with the long end of the sheet.

6. Proceed with rolling and slicing the rolls. Serve immediately.

Baked Tofu, Pickled Daikon, and Cucumber Roll

SERVES 4 | PREP TIME: 20 MINUTES

This vegetarian maki recipe features baked tofu, available at health food stores, along with pickled daikon and cucumber. You can find pickled daikon at a Japanese market or at one of the online retailers featured in the Resources section (page 163).

4 (8-by-7-inch) Toasted Nori sheets (page 52)
2 cups Sushi Rice (page 39)
8 (1-inch-wide) strips baked tofu
4 long strips pickled daikon
1 small Japanese cucumber, cut into spears

1. Follow the steps for How to Make Norimaki on page 74.

2. When directed to lay the filling, for each roll, place one quarter of the tofu, daikon, and cucumber in adjacent strips on the rice running lengthwise and parallel with the long end of the sheet.

3. Proceed with rolling and slicing the rolls. Serve immediately.

Avocado, Beet, and Pea Shoot Roll

SERVES 4 | PREP TIME: 20 MINUTES

Succulent beets make a nice visual stand-in for tuna in these colorful vegetarian rolls. You can find packaged steamed beets in the produce section of many supermarkets, or trim and quarter fresh beets and cook them in a stove top steamer for 15 minutes. Delicate pea shoots add a nice crunch and touch of dark green color to this roll.

4 (8-by-7-inch) Toasted Nori sheets (page 52)

2 cups Sushi Rice (page 39)

4 medium beets, trimmed, steamed, peeled, and cut into strips

1 medium avocado, cut into strips

1 cup pea shoots

1. Follow the steps for How to Make Norimaki on page 74.

2. When directed to lay the filling, for each roll, place one quarter of the beets, avocado, and pea shoots in adjacent strips on the rice running lengthwise and parallel with the long end of the sheet.

3. Proceed with rolling and slicing the rolls. Serve immediately.

Vegetarian Futomaki with Brown Rice

SERVES 4 | PREP TIME: 20 MINUTES

This vegetarian version of futomaki ("big roll") combines fried bean curd, pickled burdock root, pickled daikon radish, Seasoned Mushrooms (page 58), and spinach for a colorful and flavorful roll. Fried bean curd, pickled burdock root, and pickled daikon can all be purchased at a Japanese market. This recipe calls for brown sushi rice, which adds earthiness and depth to the flavor, but white sushi rice can be substituted.

4 (8-by-7-inch) Toasted Nori sheets (page 52)
2 cups Brown Sushi Rice (page 41)
8 strips fried bean curd
4 long strips pickled daikon
Seasoned Mushrooms (page 58)
4 long strips pickled burdock root
½ cup blanched spinach

1. Follow the steps for How to Make Norimaki on page 74.

2. When directed to lay the filling, for each roll, place one quarter of the fried bean curd, daikon, mushrooms, burdock, and spinach in adjacent strips in that order on the rice running lengthwise and parallel with the long end of the sheet.

3. Proceed to rolling and slicing the roll. Serve immediately.

How to Make URAMAKI

Uramaki are "inside-out" maki rolls, meaning the nori is rolled with the rice on the outside. The first uramaki was probably the California Roll, which was invented in Los Angeles in the 1960s. This special roll was meant to appease Westerners, who were wary of both raw fish and seaweed. Although uramaki looks complicated, it is just as easy to make as norimaki.

INGREDIENTS

2 (8-by-7-inch) Toasted Nori sheets (page 52), cut in half to make 4 (4-by-7-inch) sheets

Fillings (fish sliced according to the instructions for "Slicing Fish" for maki on page 46, sliced vegetables, eggs, tofu, or a combination)

2 cups Sushi Rice (page 39)

Fillings (fish roe, sliced fish, sliced vegetables, toasted sesame seeds)

2 cups water mixed with 2 tablespoons rice vinegar, for wetting hands

EQUIPMENT

Bamboo sushi-rolling mat
Plastic wrap to cover the rolling mat
Sharp knife

1 Prepare your work area by setting out your Toasted Nori sheets, Sushi Rice, fillings, toppings, and garnishes, as well as the bowl of vinegared water.

2 Lay the sushi-rolling mat on your work surface with the flat sides of the slats facing up. Cover the mat with a piece of plastic wrap.

3 Lay a sheet of nori, shiny-side up with one of the long sides facing you, on top of the plastic wrap, lined up with the edge of the mat.

4 Moisten your hands in the bowl of vinegared water; then, using your wet hands, scoop up about ½ cup of rice and press it onto the nori in an even layer about ¼-inch thick. Use your fingertips to gently distribute the rice without smashing the grains. The rice should cover the nori all the way to the edges. Pick up the nori, and turn it over on the mat so that the rice side is down.

5 Lay one quarter of the fillings in a 1½-inch-wide strip along the long edge of the nori closest to you.

6 Lift the mat at the filled edge, and gently roll it away from you until the 2 long edges are joined. Press down gently to shape the roll, using the mat to form the roll into a tight cylinder. Repeat with the remaining ingredients to form 4 rolls.

89

MAKI

continued ►

(7) If you are coating the outside of the roll with fish roe or sesame seeds, do so after the roll is formed and before slicing. With the roll on the open plastic wrap, spoon or sprinkle the topping ingredient onto the roll, spreading it with the back of the spoon if needed. Turn the roll over to coat each side. If you are topping the rolls with sliced fish or vegetables, arrange the toppings on the rolls, slightly overlapping them. Give the roll another gentle squeeze with the rolling mat to press the toppings into the rice before slicing.

(8) To slice each roll into rounds, moisten the blade of a sharp knife with water. Position the handle end of the blade crosswise at the center of the roll, and draw the knife toward you, all the way to the point, slicing through the roll in one smooth move. Repeat with the remaining 3 rolls, cutting each in half. Cut each half roll in half again using the same cutting method. Next cut each quarter in half so that you have 8 rounds for each roll.

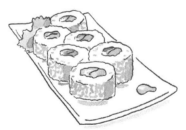

(9) Uramaki are best served immediately, but unlike with norimaki, you don't have to worry about the seaweed wrapper getting soggy, so they can be made ahead.

Tuna and Cucumber Uramaki with Black Sesame Seeds

SERVES 4 | PREP TIME: 20 MINUTES | COOK TIME: 1 MINUTE

This simple inside-out roll is filled with succulent tuna and crisp cucumber. The toasted black sesame seeds add a hint of nutty flavor, a nice crunch, and visual appeal.

2 tablespoons black sesame seeds

2 (8-by-7-inch) Toasted Nori sheets (page 52), cut in half to make 4 (4-by-7-inch) sheets

2 cups Sushi Rice (page 39)

4 ounces tuna fillet, cut into strips

1 small Japanese cucumber, cut into thin strips

1. In a small skillet over medium-high heat, toast the sesame seeds, shaking the pan frequently, just until the seeds become fragrant and begin to pop, about 1 minute. Remove the seeds from the heat immediately and transfer to a small dish.

2. Follow the steps for How to Make Uramaki on page 88.

3. When directed to lay the filling, for each roll, place one quarter of the tuna and cucumber in a 1½-inch-wide strip along the long edge of the nori closest to you.

4. Proceed to rolling. Coat the outside of each roll with one quarter of the toasted sesame seeds.

5. Slice the rolls into rounds, and serve immediately.

Salmon, Scallion, and Salmon Roe Uramaki

SERVES 4 | PREP TIME: 20 MINUTES

Fresh salmon roe (ikura) are bright red pearls about the size of a small pea. Bite into them, and they burst open, releasing a salty brine. You can buy fresh salmon roe in Japanese markets. This simple but stunning uramaki is filled with rich salmon and scallions and then garnished with salmon roe.

2 (8-by-7-inch) Toasted Nori sheets (page 52),
   cut in half to make 4 (4-by-7-inch) sheets

2 cups Sushi Rice (page 39)

4 ounces salmon fillet, cut into strips

2 scallions, sliced into 2-inch-long strips

¼ cup fresh salmon roe

1. Follow the steps for How to Make Uramaki on page 88.

2. When directed to lay the filling, for each roll, place one quarter of the salmon and scallions in a 1½-inch-wide strip along the long edge of the nori closest to you.

3. Proceed to rolling and slicing the rolls. Dollop a small spoonful of salmon roe onto each round, and serve immediately.

California Roll

SERVES 4 | PREP TIME: 20 MINUTES | COOK TIME: 1 MINUTE

Invented in Los Angeles, California, in the late 1960s, this roll is quite possibly responsible for the widespread popularity of sushi in the United States today. This first "fusion" sushi led to the creation of such beloved maki as the Rock 'n Roll (page 80), the Rainbow Roll (page 94), and the Dragon Roll (page 95), among others. It is often made with imitation crab, but using real crab is highly preferred.

2 tablespoons sesame seeds

2 (8-by-7-inch) Toasted Nori sheets (page 52), cut in half to make 4 (4-by-7-inch) sheets

2 cups Sushi Rice (page 39)

4 ounces crabmeat

1 small Japanese cucumber, cut into thin strips

1 medium avocado, cut into strips

1. In a small skillet over medium-high heat, toast the sesame seeds, shaking the pan frequently, just until the seeds become fragrant and begin to pop, about 1 minute. Remove the seeds from the heat immediately, and transfer the seeds to a small dish.

2. Follow the steps for How to Make Uramaki on page 88.

3. When directed to lay the filling, for each roll, place one quarter of the crabmeat, cucumber, and avocado in a 1½-inch-wide strip along the long edge of the nori closest to you.

4. Proceed to rolling. Coat the outside of each roll with one quarter of the toasted sesame seeds. Slice into rounds, and serve immediately.

Rainbow Roll

SERVES 4 | PREP TIME: 20 MINUTES

This is a very special roll indeed. It's a California roll inside topped with a rainbow of fish—white yellowtail, red tuna, pink salmon—plus avocado for a bit of green. Garnish the roll with a bit of tobiko (flying fish roe) if you like. Cut the fish in this recipe about 2 inches by 3 inches, according to the instruction for "Slicing Fish" for nigiri (page 48).

FOR THE CRAB SALAD

4 ounces crabmeat
2 tablespoons mayonnaise
Dash salt

FOR THE ROLLS

2 (8-by-7-inch) Toasted Nori sheets (page 52), cut in half to make 4 (4-by-7-inch) sheets
2 cups Sushi Rice (page 39)
1 small Japanese cucumber, cut into thin strips
1 medium avocado, three quarters of it cut into strips and one quarter cut into very thin pieces
4 very thin slices yellowtail
4 very thin slices salmon
4 very thin slices tuna

To make the crab salad

In a small bowl, mix the crabmeat, mayonnaise, and salt together.

To make the rolls

1. Follow the steps for How to Make Uramaki on page 88.

2. When directed to lay the filling, for each roll, place one quarter of the crab salad, cucumber, and avocado strips in a 1½-inch-wide strip along the long edge of the nori closest to you.

3. Roll up and then top each roll with 1 slice of yellowtail, 1 slice of salmon, 1 slice of tuna, and 1 thin slice of avocado. The slices should cover the whole roll. It is fine if they overlap slightly.

4. Using the rolling mat, gently press the fish onto the top of the roll. Slice and serve immediately.

Dragon Roll

SERVES 4 | PREP TIME: 40 MINUTES | COOK TIME: 5 MINUTES

This is one of the fanciest and most delicious inside-out rolls you'll find anywhere. You may also see versions of the dragon roll with eel in place of or in addition to the shrimp tempura. You'll need bamboo skewers to make the shrimp tempura.

FOR THE SHRIMP TEMPURA

2 to 3 liters neutral-flavored oil such as grapeseed or safflower

¾ cup all-purpose flour

6 tablespoons cornstarch

2¼ teaspoons baking powder

Dash salt

Dash freshly ground black pepper

8 medium shrimp, peeled and deveined (see Cooking tip, page 82)

¾ cup cold seltzer

FOR THE ROLLS

2 tablespoons black sesame seeds

2 (8-by-7-inch) Toasted Nori sheets (page 52), cut in half to make 4 (4-by-7-inch) sheets

2 cups Sushi Rice (page 39)

1 Japanese cucumber, cut into long spears

2 tablespoons flying fish roe (tobiko)

Eel Sauce (page 59)

1 large avocado, cut into thin slices

Spicy Mayo (page 60), for garnishing

To make the shrimp tempura

1. In a large, deep pot over high heat, add the oil and heat to 375°F.

2. In a medium bowl, stir together the flour, cornstarch, baking powder, salt, and pepper. Pat the shrimp dry, and dredge them in the flour mixture.

3. Spear each shrimp with a bamboo skewer from the head end to the tail in order to flatten them.

4. Whisk the seltzer into the flour mixture. Dunk each shrimp into the batter, and drop them into the hot oil. Cook for about 2 minutes, until crisp and deep golden brown all over. Drain on a paper towel-lined plate.

To make the rolls

1. In a small skillet over medium-high heat, toast the sesame seeds, shaking the pan frequently until the seeds become fragrant and begin to pop, about 1 minute. Transfer the seeds to a small dish.

2. To make the rolls, follow the steps for How to Make Uramaki on page 88.

continued ►

3. When directed to lay the filling, for each roll, place one quarter of the tempura-fried shrimp, cucumber, and flying fish roe in a 1½-inch-wide strip along the long edge of the nori closest to you.

4. Drizzle the shrimp with a bit of Eel Sauce. Roll up and then top each roll with several slices of avocado, covering the whole roll and overlapping the slices slightly.

5. Using the rolling mat, gently press the avocado onto the top of the roll. Slice the rolls, and garnish each with a dollop of Spicy Mayo and a sprinkling of toasted sesame seeds.

Cooking tip: If deep-frying the shrimp seems like too much trouble, you can defrost cooked, frozen shrimp tempura, which you can buy in Japanese markets and many supermarkets.

Ninja Roll

SERVES 4 | PREP TIME: 20 MINUTES

Made with rich yellowtail and spicy jalapeños and garnished with Spicy Mayo (page 60), this roll has a real kick. Any white fish, such as snapper or halibut, can be substituted for the yellowtail.

2 (8-by-7-inch) Toasted Nori sheets (page 52), cut in half to make 4 (4-by-7-inch) sheets

2 cups Sushi Rice (page 39)

4 ounces yellowtail, cut into strips

1 jalapeño chile, seeded and cut into very thin strips

¼ cup cilantro leaves

Spicy Mayo (page 60), for drizzling

1. Follow the steps for How to Make Uramaki on page 88.

2. When directed to lay the filling, for each roll, place one quarter of the yellowtail, chiles, and cilantro in a 1½-inch-wide strip along the long edge of the nori closest to you.

3. Proceed to rolling and slicing into rounds. Drizzle with the Spicy Mayo, and serve immediately.

Roasted Veggie Roll with Miso Sauce

SERVES 4 | PREP TIME: 30 MINUTES | COOK TIME: 10 MINUTES

Eggplant, peppers, and scallions make a healthy, colorful filling for these vegetarian rolls. Roasting the vegetables deepens their flavors and brings out their natural sweetness while the vinegary miso dipping sauce brings the perfect balance to the dish.

FOR THE MISO SAUCE

2 tablespoons mirin

2 tablespoons unseasoned rice vinegar

1 tablespoon miso paste

¼ to ½ teaspoon chile paste

FOR THE ROLLS

2 small Japanese eggplants, quartered lengthwise

2 bell peppers (orange, red, yellow, or a
   combination), seeded and quartered

4 scallions, trimmed to 8 inches in length

2 tablespoons olive oil

2 (8-by-7-inch) Toasted Nori sheets (page 52),
   cut in half to make 4 (4-by-7-inch) sheets

2 cups Sushi Rice (page 39)

To make the miso sauce

In a small bowl, stir together the mirin, vinegar, miso paste, and chile paste, mixing well.

To make the rolls

1. Preheat the broiler to medium-high.

2. In a large bowl, toss the eggplants, peppers, and scallions with the olive oil, making sure they are well coated.

3. On a baking sheet, spread the vegetables in a single layer, placing the peppers skin-side up. Place the baking sheet under the broiler. Remove the scallions after about 5 minutes, putting them on a plate to cool. Remove the eggplants when they are tender, about 2 or 3 minutes longer than the scallions. Transfer them to the plate with the scallions to cool. Continue to broil the peppers for a few minutes more, until the skins begin to blister.

4. Transfer the peppers to a medium bowl, cover, and let steam for a few minutes. Peel the skins off the peppers and cut into slices.

5. Follow the steps for How to Make Uramaki on page 88.

6. When directed to lay the filling, for each roll, place one quarter of the eggplant, scallions, and peppers in a 1½-inch-wide strip along the long edge of the nori closest to you.

7. Proceed to rolling and slicing into rounds. Serve immediately with the miso sauce for dipping.

Cooking tip: If you can't find Japanese eggplants, use a regular eggplant and cut it into thin (½-inch) strips.

Seasoned Mushroom, Radish Sprouts, and Asparagus Roll

SERVES 4 | PREP TIME: 20 MINUTES | COOK TIME: 1 MINUTE

Radish sprouts (kaiware) are the sprouts of the Japanese daikon radish. They have a peppery flavor and pretty green leaves that add freshness to this vegetarian roll. You can find radish sprouts in Asian markets, but if they aren't available, substitute pea shoots or other sprouts.

4 fat spears or 8 thin spears asparagus, trimmed
2 (8-by-7-inch) Toasted Nori sheets (page 52),
   cut in half to make 4 (4-by-7-inch) sheets
2 cups Sushi Rice (page 39)
Seasoned Mushrooms (page 58)
½ cup radish sprouts

1. Prepare a medium bowl of ice water. In a medium pot over medium-high heat, add enough lightly salted water to cover the asparagus by a few inches, and bring the water to a boil. Add the asparagus and cook for 1 minute. Using tongs or a slotted spoon, transfer the asparagus to the ice water bath and let chill for a few minutes. Drain the asparagus and pat dry. Set aside.

2. Follow the steps for How to Make Uramaki on page 88.

3. When directed to lay the filling, for each roll, place one quarter of the mushrooms, asparagus, and radish sprouts in a 1½-inch-wide strip along the long edge of the nori closest to you.

4. Proceed to rolling and slicing into rounds. Serve immediately.

How to Make TEMAKI

Temaki are hand-rolled, cone-shaped, nori-wrapped sushi filled with rice and fish or vegetable fillings. They are ideal for a DIY sushi bar: Set out a selection of fillings and sushi rice, and let guests roll their own.

INGREDIENTS

4 (8-by-7-inch) Toasted Nori sheets (page 52), cut in half to make 8 (3½-by-8-inch) sheets

2 cups Sushi Rice (page 39)

Fillings (fish sliced according to the instructions on "Slicing Fish" for maki on page 46, but cut into 2- or 3-inch lengths, sliced vegetables, eggs, tofu, or a combination)

2 cups water mixed with 2 tablespoons rice vinegar, for wetting hands

1 Prepare your work area by setting out your nori sheets, sushi rice, fillings, and toppings, as well as the bowl of vinegared water.

2 Lay a half sheet of nori, shiny-side down, on your work surface with the long side toward you.

continued ►

101

MAKI

3 Moisten your hands in the bowl of vinegared water; then, using your wet hands, scoop up about ¼ cup of rice and press it onto the left-hand side of the nori. Using your fingertips, press the rice into an even layer, about ¼-inch thick, covering the left third of the nori. Leave a ½-inch rice-free border along the long edge closest to you.

4 Lay one quarter of the fillings diagonally across the rectangle of rice, from the lower right-hand corner to the upper left-hand corner of the rice, being careful not to overfill the roll.

5 Place one grain of rice in the lower right-hand corner of the nori sheet.

6 Dry your hands well so that they don't stick to the nori or make it soggy. Fold the left-hand corner of the nori up and over the diagonal line of fillings so that the lower right-hand corner of the rice square becomes a point. Continue to roll the nori into a cone shape that holds the fillings securely.

7 To seal the cone, press down on the nori over the single grain of rice in the tip.

8 Serve immediately. Storing temaki is not recommended, because the nori becomes soggy and the rice will become hard if refrigerated.

Smoked Salmon, Avocado, Cucumber, and Scallion Temaki

MAKES 4 ROLLS | PREP TIME: 10 MINUTES

Smoked salmon is a good compromise between raw and cooked fish if you either don't have access to sushi-quality raw fish or are squeamish about it. Either way, lox is delicious paired with fatty avocado, crisp cucumber, and sharp scallions.

2 (8-by-7-inch) Toasted Nori sheets (page 52), cut in half to make 4 (3½-by-8-inch) sheets

1 cup Sushi Rice (page 39)

2 ounces smoked salmon, cut into 8 strips

½ small avocado, sliced thin

½ small cucumber, cut into thin 4-inch-long strips

2 scallions, cut into thin 4-inch strips

1. Follow the steps for How to Make Temaki on page 101.

2. When directed to lay the filling, for each roll, place one quarter of the salmon, avocado, cucumber, and scallions diagonally across the rectangle of rice, from the lower right-hand corner to the upper left-hand corner of the rice, being careful not to overfill the roll.

3. Proceed with rolling. Serve immediately.

Tuna, Chile-Daikon Relish, and Radish Sprout Temaki

MAKES 4 ROLLS | PREP TIME: 10 MINUTES

Crisp Chile-Daikon Relish (page 54) is a perfect counterpoint to rich, meaty tuna. Including the peppery, fresh daikon radish sprouts adds a nice green element. You can buy radish sprouts in Asian markets or substitute pea shoots or another type of sprout.

2 (8-by-7-inch) Toasted Nori sheets (page 52), cut in half to make 4 (3½-by-8-inch) sheets
1 cup Sushi Rice (page 39)
2 ounces tuna fillet, cut into 8 strips
¼ cup Chile-Daikon Relish (page 54)
½ cup radish sprouts

1. Follow the steps for How to Make Temaki on page 101.

2. When directed to lay the filling, for each roll, place one quarter of the tuna, Chile-Daikon Relish, and sprouts diagonally across the rectangle of rice, from the lower right-hand corner to the upper left-hand corner of the rice, being careful not to overfill the roll.

3. Proceed with rolling. Serve immediately.

Crab, Mango, and Cilantro Temaki

MAKES 4 ROLLS | PREP TIME: 10 MINUTES

Mango is a nontraditional sushi ingredient, but its sweet flavor and tender texture pair beautifully with rich crabmeat. Cilantro adds bright flavor and color, making this a festive roll.

2 (8-by-7-inch) Toasted Nori (page 52) sheets, cut in half to make 4 (3½-by-8-inch) sheets
1 cup Sushi Rice (page 39)
3 ounces crabmeat
½ small mango, thinly sliced
½ cup cilantro

1. Follow the steps for How to Make Temaki on page 101.

2. When directed to lay the filling, for each roll, place one quarter of the crabmeat, mango, and cilantro diagonally across the rectangle of rice, from the lower right-hand corner to the upper left-hand corner of the rice, being careful not to overfill the roll.

3. Proceed with rolling. Serve immediately.

Green Bean, Baked Tofu, and Spinach Temaki with Ochazuke Wakame

MAKES 4 ROLLS | PREP TIME: 15 MINUTES | COOK TIME: 2 MINUTES

Ochazuke Wakame (also called Wakame Chazuke) is a seasoning mix usually sprinkled over rice. It is made of dried seaweed and crispy rice balls. In this recipe it adds saltiness, umami, and a delightful crunch to a vegetarian temaki. It is sold in jars in Japanese markets.

12 thin green beans, trimmed

4 cups fresh spinach leaves

2 (8-by-7-inch) Toasted Nori sheets (page 52), cut in half to make 4 (3½-by-8-inch) sheets

1 cup Sushi Rice (page 39)

3 ounces baked tofu, cut into strips

4 teaspoons ochazuke wakame

1. Prepare a medium bowl of ice water. In a medium pot over medium-high heat, add enough lightly salted water to cover the green beans by a few inches, and bring the water to a boil. Add the green beans, and cook for 1 minute. Using tongs or a slotted spoon, transfer the green beans to the ice water bath and let chill for a few minutes. Drain and pat dry. Set aside.

2. Bring the green bean water back to a boil, add the spinach, and cook just until wilted, about 20 seconds. Remove with a slotted spoon, and drain well on paper towels.

3. Follow the steps for How to Make Temaki on page 101.

4. When directed to lay the filling, for each roll, place one quarter of the green beans, spinach, and tofu diagonally across the rectangle of rice, from the lower right-hand corner to the upper left-hand corner of the rice, being careful not to overfill the roll.

5. Sprinkle 1 teaspoon of ochazuke wakame over the filling in each roll, proceed with rolling, and serve immediately.

Kale, Sweet Potato, and Avocado Temaki

MAKES 4 ROLLS | PREP TIME: 15 MINUTES | COOK TIME: 4 MINUTES

Bright orange sweet potato brings vivid color to this vegetarian roll. The sweetness of the potato pairs nicely with salty soy sauce and the kick of wasabi, so be sure to serve both alongside for dipping.

½ small sweet potato, peeled and cut into sticks
2 (8-by-7-inch) Toasted Nori sheets (page 52),
　　cut in half to make 4 (3½-by-8-inch) sheets
1 cup Sushi Rice (page 39)
2 tender kale leaves, very finely julienned
½ medium avocado, thinly sliced

1. In a medium saucepan, bring lightly salted water (enough to cover the sweet potato by a few inches) to a boil over high heat. Add the sweet potato and cook just until tender, about 4 minutes. Drain and set aside to cool.

2. Follow the steps for How to Make Temaki on page 101.

3. When directed to lay the filling, for each roll, place one quarter of the sweet potato, kale, and avocado diagonally across the rectangle of rice, from the lower right-hand corner to the upper left-hand corner of the rice, being careful not to overfill the roll.

4. Proceed with rolling. Serve immediately.

TEMARI SUSHI RICE BALLS

7

Temari, meaning "hand ball," gets its name from the colorful folk art balls made of scraps of kimono fabric and embroidered in stunning designs. ▣ Because temari sushi are so easy to make, they are popular with home cooks. The only equipment you'll need to form these rice balls is a piece of plastic wrap. Like temaki, these are a great choice for a DIY sushi bar—just set out rice, toppings, and squares of plastic wrap and let guests get creative. ▣ Raw fish and vegetables such as cucumber or avocado work especially well with temari because they can be sliced thin and molded artfully around the rice. Garnish with fish roe, sauces, snipped chives, and other decorative touches. Use contrasting colors (pink salmon and green avocado) or layer translucent, paper-thin slices of fish over other ingredients for an interesting presentation. Use nori strips to tie the toppings onto the rice ball or salmon roe to dot the tops. Whatever you put on your rice balls, they are bound to look festive and taste delicious!

How to Make TEMARI

Temari are small balls of rice, about the size of a golf ball, with assorted toppings. Using a piece of plastic wrap makes it easy to form the ingredients into pretty balls of uniform shape and size.

INGREDIENTS

Sushi Rice (page 39)

Toppings (fish, sliced according to the instructions for "Slicing Fish" for temari on page 48, sliced vegetables, omelet, tofu, or a combination)

Garnishes (fish roe, toasted sesame seeds, sauces, scallion ribbons, chives, radish sprouts, thin strips of nori)

2 cups water mixed with 2 tablespoons rice vinegar, for wetting hands

EQUIPMENT

Plastic wrap cut into an 8-inch square

1 Prepare your work area by setting out your Sushi Rice, toppings, and garnishes, as well as the bowl of vinegared water.

2 On a smooth surface, lay down your plastic wrap square and then place the topping or toppings (as noted in individual recipes) in the center of the plastic wrap.

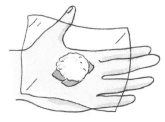

3 Wet your hands with the vinegared water, and scoop up about 1½ tablespoons of rice. Form the rice into a ball with your hands. Place the ball on the topping on the plastic wrap.

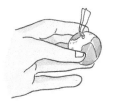

4 Bring all sides of the plastic wrap up around the ball of rice and twist to make a tight bundle. Gently press the topping into the rice while twisting the plastic wrap to pack the ball so that it is nice and round and holds together.

5 Remove the plastic wrap, garnish as desired, and serve immediately.

Tuna and Cucumber Temari
with Scallions

MAKES ABOUT 10 RICE BALLS | PREP TIME: 15 MINUTES

Pale, delicate cucumber provides a visual and textural contrast to rich, meaty red tuna. Wasabi paste and scallions add even more color and flavor. You'll need about 2 ounces of fish for this recipe.

1 cup Sushi Rice (page 39)
10 (⅛ inch-thick) slices tuna, about
   1½-by-1½-inches square
½ small Japanese cucumber, sliced into
   10 (2-by-1-by-⅛-inch) pieces
1 tablespoon wasabi paste
2 scallions, white and light green parts sliced
   paper thin

1. Follow the steps for How to Make Temari on page 110.

2. When directed to place the topping, for each ball, lay 1 strip of tuna and 1 strip of cucumber side by side in the center of the plastic wrap square.

3. Proceed to form the rice ball, place it on top of the tuna and cucumber, and use the plastic wrap to form a ball.

4. Remove the plastic wrap, and add a small dollop of wasabi paste to the top of each ball. Garnish with a few slices of scallion. Serve immediately.

Salmon and Avocado Temari with Salmon Roe

MAKES ABOUT 10 RICE BALLS | PREP TIME: 15 MINUTES

Rich, flavorful salmon and creamy avocado are a match made in heaven. Bright orange pearls of salmon roe add a pop, both visually and flavor-wise. You'll need about 2 ounces of fish for this recipe.

1 cup Sushi Rice (page 39)
10 (⅛-inch-thick) slices salmon, about
    1½-by-1½-inches square
½ medium avocado, sliced into
    10 (2-by-1-by-⅛-inch) pieces
2 tablespoons salmon roe

1. Follow the steps for How to Make Temari on page 110.

2. When directed to place the topping, for each ball, lay 1 strip of salmon and 1 strip of avocado side by side in the center of the plastic wrap square.

3. Proceed to form the rice ball, place it on top of the salmon and avocado, and use the plastic wrap to form a ball.

4. Remove the plastic wrap, and add a spoonful of salmon roe to the top of each ball. Serve immediately.

Shrimp Temari with Radish Sprouts

MAKES ABOUT 10 RICE BALLS | PREP TIME: 15 MINUTES | COOK TIME: 2 MINUTES

Halved pink shrimp naturally curl around each other in an artful way. Peppery radish sprouts add a little kick, but feel free to add a smear of wasabi to the top of the rice ball before placing it on the shrimp if you like.

10 medium shrimp, heads removed and deveined (see Cooking tip, page 82)
1 cup Sushi Rice (page 39)
2 tablespoons radish sprouts

1. In a large saucepan or stockpot (wide enough to hold the skewers) over medium-high heat, bring the shrimp and enough salted water (about 1 tablespoon salt) to cover the shrimp to a boil. Cook for about 2 minutes, until the shrimp is pink and opaque. Remove the shrimp from the water and let cool. Once the shrimp is cool enough to handle, remove the shells. Using a sharp knife, cut the shrimp lengthwise, splitting each into two pieces.

2. Follow the steps for How to Make Temari on page 110.

3. When directed to place the topping, for each ball, lay 2 halves of a shrimp in the center of the plastic wrap square in a yin-yang fashion, cut-side up.

4. Proceed to form the rice ball, place it on top of the shrimp, and use the plastic wrap to form a ball.

5. Remove the plastic wrap, and arrange a bit of radish sprouts on top of each, nestled between the two shrimp halves. Serve immediately.

Yellowtail and Red Chili Temari with Ponzu Dipping Sauce

MAKES ABOUT 10 RICE BALLS | PREP TIME: 15 MINUTES

Slicing the yellowtail paper thin makes it translucent, allowing a slice of red chile placed beneath it to show through. Use a mandoline or a very sharp knife to slice the chile very thinly. Serve with Ponzu Dipping Sauce (page 61). You'll need about 2 ounces of fish for this recipe.

1 cup Sushi Rice (page 39)

10 paper-thin slices yellowtail, about 1½-by-1½-inches square

1 large red jalapeño chile, seeded and sliced into paper-thin rounds

Ponzu Dipping Sauce (page 61)

1. Follow the steps for How to Make Temari on page 110.

2. When directed to place the topping, for each ball, lay 1 square of yellowtail in the center of the plastic wrap square and top it with 1 or more thin slices of chile.

3. Proceed to form the rice ball, place it on top of the yellowtail and chile, and use the plastic wrap to form a ball.

4. Remove the plastic wrap, and serve immediately with Ponzu Dipping Sauce alongside.

Smoked Salmon Temari
with Lemon-Wasabi Sauce

MAKES ABOUT 10 RICE BALLS | PREP TIME: 15 MINUTES

Smoked salmon is a favorite of people who don't care for raw fish. Here it gets a blast of flavor from Lemon-Wasabi Sauce (page 62). This would be a great sushi to serve as part of a Sunday brunch. Garnish with snipped chives or thinly sliced scallions if you like. You'll need about 2 ounces of fish for this recipe.

1 cup Sushi Rice (page 39)
10 thin slices smoked salmon, about
   1½-by-1½-inches square
Lemon-Wasabi Sauce (page 62)

1. Follow the steps for How to Make Temari on page 110.

2. When directed to place the topping, for each ball, lay 1 square of smoked salmon in the center of the plastic wrap square.

3. Proceed to form the rice ball, place it on top of the smoked salmon, and use the plastic wrap to form a ball.

4. Remove the plastic wrap, drizzle the ball with Lemon-Wasabi Sauce, and serve immediately.

Crab Salad Temari with Flying Fish Roe

MAKES ABOUT 10 RICE BALLS | PREP TIME: 15 MINUTES

Crab salad makes a decadent topping for temari. Tiny, bright orange flying fish roe add a spot of color and a nice, salty crunch. You can make this into a spicy crab temari by substituting Spicy Mayo (page 60) for the regular mayonnaise.

⅔ cup crabmeat

1½ tablespoons mayonnaise

1 cup Sushi Rice (page 39)

3 tablespoons flying fish roe

1. In a small bowl, stir together the crabmeat and mayonnaise.

2. Follow the steps for How to Make Temari on page 110.

3. When directed to place the topping, for each ball, place about 1 teaspoon of the flying fish roe and 1 tablespoon of the crabmeat mixture side by side in the center of the plastic wrap square.

4. Proceed to form the rice ball, place it on top of the flying fish roe and crabmeat mixture, and use the plastic wrap to form a ball.

5. Remove the plastic wrap, and serve immediately.

Omelet and Roasted Red Pepper Temari

MAKES ABOUT 10 RICE BALLS | PREP TIME: 15 MINUTES

Japanese omelet (tamago) is slightly sweet, so it pairs beautifully with the sweet, earthy flavor of roasted red peppers. Freshly roasted peppers have the best flavor, but if you don't have time, you can always substitute roasted peppers from a jar.

1 red bell pepper, seeded and quartered

2 teaspoons olive oil

10 (⅛-inch-thick) slices Omelet (page 56), about 1½ inches by 1 inch

1 cup Sushi Rice (page 39)

1. Preheat the broiler to medium-high.

2. Brush the red pepper all over with the olive oil.

3. Place the red pepper on a baking sheet, skin-side up, and cook it under the broiler until the skin begins to blister and blacken, about 5 minutes. Transfer the pepper to a bowl, cover, and let steam for a few minutes. Peel the skins off the peppers and cut into 10 (1½-by-1-inch) squares.

4. Follow the steps for How to Make Temari on page 110.

5. When directed to place the topping, for each ball, place a slice of omelet and a slice of roasted pepper side by side in the center of the plastic wrap square.

6. Proceed to form the rice ball, place it on top of the omelet and roasted red pepper, and use the plastic wrap to form a ball.

7. Remove the plastic wrap, and serve immediately.

Pickled Daikon Radish and Seasoned Mushroom Temari

MAKES ABOUT 10 RICE BALLS | PREP TIME: 15 MINUTES

This vegetarian temari gets a vinegary tang—not to mention a nice crunch—from the pickled daikon radish and tons of umami from the Seasoned Mushrooms (page 58). You can buy pickled daikon radish in Japanese or Asian markets.

10 (⅛-inch-thick) slices pickled daikon radish, about 1½ inches by 1 inch
10 slices Seasoned Mushrooms (page 58)
1 cup Sushi Rice (page 39)

1. Follow the steps for How to Make Temari on page 110.

2. When directed to place the topping, for each ball, lay a slice of pickled radish and a slice of mushroom side by side in the center of the plastic wrap square.

3. Proceed to form the rice ball, place it on top of the radish and mushroom, and use the plastic wrap to form a ball.

4. Remove the plastic wrap, and serve immediately.

NIGIRI HAND-FORMED SUSHI
GUNKANMAKI BATTLESHIP SUSHI

8

Nigiri is the ultimate sushi—the preparation that Japanese sushi chefs train for years to make. In this chapter, you'll learn the proper technique for scooping up rice and forming it into a neat oval, one that holds together between chopsticks but gently breaks apart in your mouth. It all comes together with a delicate smear of wasabi and a perfectly cut slice of fish, omelet, or vegetable. ▣ *Gunkanmaki*, or battleship sushi, is similar to nigiri in that it starts with a hand-formed oval of rice, but instead of placing a topping directly on the rice, a strip of nori is first wrapped around the rice ball, creating a wall to hold in toppings. The wrapped oval shape is similar to a boat, giving rise to its name.

How to Make NIGIRI

Nigiri are bite-size, hand-formed rice balls topped with fish or vegetables. No special equipment is needed, just deft hands.

INGREDIENTS

2 cups Sushi Rice (page 39)

Toppings (fish, sliced according to the instructions for "Slicing Fish" for nigiri, on page 48, or vegetables or eggs, cut into a similar size and shape)

2 cups water mixed with 2 tablespoons rice vinegar, for wetting hands

Wasabi (if using)

1 Prepare your work area by setting out your Sushi Rice, sliced toppings, and garnishes, as well as the bowl of vinegared water.

2 Moisten your hands in the bowl of vinegared water, and then, using your wet hands, scoop up about 2 tablespoons of rice in your palm. Use two fingers of your other hand to press the rice into an oval about 1 inch wide and 2 inches long. Pack the rice together tightly enough that it won't fall apart when lifted with chopsticks.

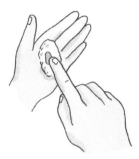

3 Using a chopstick or the tip of your finger, spread a small amount of wasabi onto the rice, if desired.

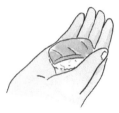

4 Place a slice of fish or other topping on top of the rice, draping it over the ends. Press gently to make sure the topping sticks to the rice.

5 Repeat steps 2 through 4 until all the rice and toppings are gone. Serve immediately. Storing nigiri is not recommended, because the rice will become hard if refrigerated.

Tuna Nigiri

MAKES ABOUT 16 NIGIRI | PREP TIME: 15 MINUTES

This is the quintessential nigiri sushi—just melt-in-your-mouth, meaty tuna over perfectly seasoned sushi rice. You can use ahi, yellowfin, bluefin, or bigeye tuna. Shiso (also called perilla) is a Japanese herb in the mint family with an intriguing herbaceous flavor. Its bright, almost citrusy flavor is a good match for meaty, rich tuna, which is why they are commonly paired in sushi or sashimi dishes.

2 cups Sushi Rice (page 39)

2 tablespoons wasabi paste (optional)

16 small fresh shiso leaves (optional)

6 ounces tuna fillet, sliced according to the instructions for "Slicing Fish" for nigiri (page 48)

1. Follow the steps for How to Make Nigiri on page 122.

2. After tightly packing each rice ball and smearing it with a bit of wasabi paste (if desired), top each with a shiso leaf (if using) and a slice of tuna, draping the toppings over the ends of the rice. Press gently to make sure the toppings stick to the rice.

3. Serve immediately.

Salmon Nigiri with Wasabi

MAKES ABOUT 16 NIGIRI | PREP TIME: 15 MINUTES

There are many different species of salmon, but king salmon is the most popular among sushi chefs because of its ideal fat content and superior texture. When available, choose wild salmon over farmed, as it is more flavorful and healthier.

2 cups Sushi Rice (page 39)

6 ounces salmon fillet, sliced according to the instructions for "Slicing Fish" for nigiri (page 48)

2 tablespoons wasabi paste

1. Follow the steps for How to Make Nigiri on page 122.

2. After tightly packing each rice ball and smearing it with a bit of wasabi paste, top each with a slice of salmon, draping it over the ends of the rice. Press gently to make sure the salmon sticks to the rice.

3. Serve immediately.

Yellowtail Nigiri with Scallion

MAKES ABOUT 16 NIGIRI | PREP TIME: 15 MINUTES

Yellowtail (hamachi) is a type of amberjack. Its meat is pale and rich in oil, its texture smooth and buttery, and its flavor rich without being at all fishy. Many connoisseurs prefer it to tuna for sushi and sashimi.

2 cups Sushi Rice (page 39)

2 tablespoons wasabi paste (optional)

6 ounces yellowtail fillet, sliced according to the instructions for "Slicing Fish" for nigiri (page 48)

3 scallions, white and light green parts very thinly sliced

1. Follow the steps for How to Make Nigiri on page 122.

2. After tightly packing each rice ball and smearing it with a bit of wasabi paste (if using), top each with a slice of yellowtail, draping it over the ends of the rice, and garnish with sliced scallions. Press gently to make sure the yellowtail sticks to the rice.

3. Serve immediately.

Snapper Nigiri
with Ponzu Dipping Sauce

MAKES ABOUT 16 NIGIRI | PREP TIME: 15 MINUTES

Snapper (tai) is a delicate, mildly flavored white fish. True snapper is especially prized by sushi chefs, but it is difficult to find in the United States. Other types of snapper or similar red fish (such as rockfish) can be substituted.

2 cups Sushi Rice (page 39)
6 ounces snapper fillet, sliced according to the instructions for "Slicing Fish" for nigiri (page 48)
2 tablespoons wasabi paste (optional)
Ponzu Dipping Sauce (page 61)

1. Follow the steps for How to Make Nigiri on page 122.

2. After tightly packing each rice ball and smearing it with a bit of wasabi paste (if using), top each with a slice of snapper, draping it over the ends of the rice. Press gently to make sure the snapper sticks to the rice.

3. Serve immediately with Ponzu Dipping Sauce.

Salmon Nigiri with Lemon and Sea Salt

MAKES ABOUT 16 NIGIRI | PREP TIME: 15 MINUTES

Lemon and coarse sea salt balance the richness of succulent salmon. Its beautiful pink color makes it especially visually appealing. Salmon is one fish that really must be flash frozen before serving raw since it can contain parasites.

2 cups Sushi Rice (page 39)
2 tablespoons wasabi paste (optional)
6 ounces salmon fillet, sliced according to the
   instructions for "Slicing Fish" for nigiri (page 48)
Juice of ½ lemon
Coarse sea salt

1. Follow the steps for How to Make Nigiri on page 122.

2. After tightly packing each rice ball and smearing it with a bit of wasabi paste (if using), top each with a slice of salmon, draping it over the ends of the rice. Press gently to make sure the salmon sticks to the rice.

3. Just before serving, squeeze a bit of lemon juice over the nigiri and sprinkle with sea salt. Serve immediately.

Poached Shrimp Nigiri with Wasabi

MAKES ABOUT 16 NIGIRI | PREP TIME: 15 MINUTES | COOK TIME: 2 MINUTES

Poaching shrimp with the shells on is the best way to maintain their sweet flavor and plump texture. When poaching shrimp for sushi, thread them onto bamboo skewers before cooking so that they will remain flat instead of curling up. For this recipe, you'll need 16 bamboo skewers.

16 medium shrimp, heads removed and deveined (see Cooking tip, page 82)
2 cups Sushi Rice (page 39)
2 tablespoons wasabi paste

1. In a large saucepan or stockpot (it should be wide enough to hold the skewers) over medium-high heat, bring enough salted water to cover the shrimp to a boil.

2. Insert a bamboo skewer through each shrimp from the head end straight through to the tail so that the shrimp is flat. Place the skewered shrimp in the boiling water and cook for about 2 minutes, until the shrimp is pink and opaque. Remove the shrimp from the water and let cool.

3. Once the shrimp is cool enough to handle, remove the shells. Using a sharp knife, butterfly the shrimp by cutting along the inner curve, being careful not to cut all the way through the flesh.

4. Follow the steps for How to Make Nigiri on page 122.

5. After tightly packing each rice ball and smearing it with a bit of wasabi paste, top each with a butterflied shrimp, cut-side down. Press gently to make sure the shrimp sticks to the rice.

6. Serve immediately.

Soy-Cured Tuna Nigiri with Jalapeño

MAKES ABOUT 16 NIGIRI | PREP TIME: 15 MINUTES, PLUS 45 MINUTES TO MARINATE | COOK TIME: 1 MINUTE

In Japan, marinated or cured tuna is known as maguro zuke. This traditional recipe, which originated in Tokyo, infuses the tuna with soy flavor, while the inside remains succulent and raw. Minced jalapeño chile adds a bit of a kick.

3 tablespoons soy sauce

1 tablespoon mirin

1 tablespoon sake

½ small jalapeño chile, seeded and finely diced

1 (6-ounce) tuna fillet

2 cups Sushi Rice (page 39)

1. In a small saucepan over medium heat, bring the soy sauce, mirin, and sake to a boil. Let boil for 1 minute, then remove from the heat, add the diced jalapeño, and cool completely. (The marinade can be refrigerated at this point.)

2. In a dish just large enough to hold the tuna fillet, pour the cooled soy sauce mixture over the top of the fish. Cover and refrigerate for 45 minutes, turning the fish over once halfway through.

3. Remove the fish from the marinade (discard the marinade), and slice the fish according to the instructions for "Slicing Fish" for nigiri (page 48).

4. Follow the steps for How to Make Nigiri on page 122.

5. After tightly packing each rice ball, top each with a slice of the marinated tuna, draping it over the ends of the rice. Press gently to make sure the tuna sticks to the rice.

6. Serve immediately.

Seared Tuna Nigiri with Wasabi Mayo

MAKES ABOUT 16 NIGIRI | PREP TIME: 15 MINUTES, PLUS 1 HOUR TO MARINATE | COOK TIME: 4 MINUTES

Marinating tuna in soy sauce, sesame oil, and ginger and then searing it over high heat gives it tons of flavor. This dish requires very fresh, sushi-quality tuna since only the very edge is cooked while the inside remains raw.

FOR THE NIGIRI

2 tablespoons sesame oil

2 tablespoons soy sauce

1 teaspoon grated fresh ginger

⅛ teaspoon garlic powder

1 (6-ounce) tuna steak, about 1½ to 2 inches thick

2 cups Sushi Rice (page 39)

FOR THE WASABI MAYO

3 tablespoons mayonnaise

1 teaspoon wasabi paste

To make the nigiri

1. In a small bowl, stir together the sesame oil, soy sauce, ginger, and garlic.

2. In a nonreactive container, pour the marinade over the tuna. Turn the tuna over to coat. Cover and refrigerate for 1 hour.

3. Heat a medium skillet over medium-high heat until very hot. Remove the tuna from the marinade, and pat dry with paper towels. Place the tuna in the pan and cook for about 1 minute per side, turning to cook all sides.

4. Slice the tuna according to the instructions for "Slicing Fish" for nigiri (page 48).

5. Follow the steps for How to Make Nigiri on page 122.

6. After tightly packing each rice ball, top each with a slice of tuna, draping it over the ends of the rice. Press gently to make sure the tuna sticks to the rice.

To make the wasabi mayo and serve

In a small bowl, stir together the mayonnaise and wasabi paste, mixing well. Add a dollop of the wasabi mayonnaise to the top of each piece of nigiri, and serve immediately.

Avocado, Cucumber, and Shiso Nigiri

MAKES ABOUT 16 NIGIRI | PREP TIME: 15 MINUTES

Shiso, a member of the mint family, combines beautifully here with refreshing cucumber and creamy avocado, both in flavor and by adorning the nigiri with three shades of green. If you can't find shiso leaves, you can substitute basil.

2 cups Sushi Rice (page 39)

2 tablespoons wasabi paste (optional)

16 thin slices avocado

16 thin half-moon slices cucumber

8 large shiso leaves, halved diagonally

1. Follow the steps for How to Make Nigiri on page 122.

2. After tightly packing each rice ball and smearing it with a bit of wasabi paste (if using), top each with a slice of avocado and a slice of cucumber, overlapping them slightly. Wrap a shiso leaf around the middle of the nigiri with the ends tucked underneath. Press gently to make sure the toppings stick to the rice.

3. Serve immediately.

Dashimaki Tamago Nigiri with Pickled Ginger

MAKES ABOUT 16 NIGIRI | PREP TIME: 15 MINUTES

Because the omelet is slightly sweet, many people like to have this nigiri as the last bite of their meal. Using pickled ginger in nigiri isn't common, but here it cuts the richness of the egg nicely.

2 cups Sushi Rice (page 39)

16 strips pickled ginger

1 Omelet (page 56),
   cut into 16 (½-inch-thick) rectangles

16 strips Toasted Nori (page 52), cut into
   ¾-inch-by-4-inch strips

1. Follow the steps for How to Make Nigiri on page 122.

2. After tightly packing each rice ball, top each with a slice of ginger and then a slice of omelet, draping them over the ends of the rice. Press gently to make sure the toppings stick to the rice.

3. Dry your hands well. Wrap a strip of nori around the belly of the nigiri, tucking the ends under the bottom. Moisten the two ends of the strip with a bit of water on your finger, and seal. Serve immediately.

Seasoned Mushroom Nigiri with Chives

MAKES ABOUT 16 NIGIRI | PREP TIME: 15 MINUTES

Seasoned mushrooms are full of umami, making this a satisfying vegetarian nigiri option. Chives add a bright counterpoint to the earthiness of the mushrooms, bringing depth to this simple recipe.

2 cups Sushi Rice (page 39)
16 strips Seasoned Mushrooms (page 58)
16 strips chives

1. Follow the steps for How to Make Nigiri on page 122.

2. After tightly packing each rice ball, top each with a strip of mushroom, draping it over the ends of the rice.

3. Wrap a chive around the belly of the nigiri, crossing it on top to tie it. Serve immediately.

How to Make GUNKANMAKI

Gunkanmaki means "battleship rolls." They are boat-shaped, hand-formed rice balls wrapped with a strip of nori to form a container that can hold loose or minced toppings.

INGREDIENTS

1 cup Sushi Rice (page 39)

8 strips Toasted Nori (page 52), about 1 inch by 7 inches

Toppings (fish roe, seafood salad, seaweed salad, minced and cooked vegetables)

2 cups water mixed with 2 tablespoons rice vinegar, for wetting hands

1 Prepare your work area by setting out your Sushi Rice, Toasted Nori strips, toppings, and garnishes, as well as the bowl of vinegared water.

2 Moisten your hands in the bowl of vinegared water, and then, using your wet hands, scoop up about 2 tablespoons of rice into your palm. Using two fingers of your other hand, press the rice into an oval about 1 inch wide and 2 inches long. Pack the rice together tightly enough that it won't fall apart when lifted with chopsticks. Make several rice balls.

continued ▶

3 Dry your hands well. Wrap the nori strips around the perimeter of the rice balls. Moisten the overlapping ends with a bit of water to seal them.

5 Serve immediately. Storing gunkanmaki is not recommended, because the nori will become soggy and the rice will become hard if refrigerated.

4 Spoon the filling into the boat as instructed in each of the individual recipes, and add any garnishes.

Tobiko Gunkanmaki with Quail Egg

MAKES 8 GUNKANMAKI | PREP TIME: 15 MINUTES

A small but rich quail egg yolk adds a creamy contrast to the salty, crunchy fish roe. Quail eggs can be purchased at most Asian markets as well as at many farmers' markets or natural food stores. You can substitute just about any type of fish roe you like here—such as salmon or herring—for the flying fish roe. Some Japanese markets sell flying fish roe flavored with wasabi, yuzu, or chiles, which would make for an interesting twist here.

1 cup Sushi Rice (page 39)
8 strips Toasted Nori (page 52), about 1 inch
   by 7 inches
½ cup flying fish roe
8 quail eggs (raw)

1. Follow the steps for How to Make Gunkanmaki on page 135 to form the nori-wrapped rice balls.

2. Spoon about a tablespoon of flying fish roe onto each wrapped rice ball.

3. Separate the egg yolks from the whites (discard the whites), and place one yolk on top of each boat.

4. Serve immediately.

Spicy Crab Salad Gunkanmaki with Black Sesame Seeds

MAKES 8 GUNKANMAKI | PREP TIME: 15 MINUTES

The boat shape of gunkanmaki makes them the perfect vessel for this spicy crab salad, which would never stay put on top of nigiri. Toasted black sesame seeds add a nice crunch and a hint of nutty flavor.

FOR THE SPICY CRAB SALAD

½ cup crabmeat
1 tablespoon Spicy Mayo (page 60)

FOR THE GUNKANMAKI

1 tablespoon black sesame seeds
1 cup Sushi Rice (page 39)
8 strips Toasted Nori (page 52), about 1 inch by 7 inches

To make the spicy crab salad

In a small bowl, stir together the crabmeat and Spicy Mayo, mixing well.

To make the gunkanmaki

1. In a small skillet over medium-high heat, toast the sesame seeds, shaking the pan frequently, just until the seeds become fragrant and begin to pop, about 1 minute. Remove the seeds from the heat immediately and transfer to a small dish.

2. Follow the steps for How to Make Gunkanmaki on page 135 to form the nori-wrapped rice balls.

3. Spoon about a tablespoon of crab salad into each boat.

4. Garnish with toasted sesame seeds, and serve immediately.

Miso Scallops Gunkanmaki

MAKES 8 GUNKANMAKI | PREP TIME: 15 MINUTES

Umami-rich miso and sweet mirin make a perfect sauce for delicate scallops. If you can't find fresh scallops, make sure you buy "dry pack" scallops—packed without chemical additives— to ensure good flavor.

1 tablespoon white miso paste

1½ teaspoons sugar

½ teaspoon mirin

1 tablespoon vinegar

½ teaspoon Dijon mustard

3 ounces scallops, diced

1 cup Sushi Rice (page 39)

8 strips Toasted Nori (page 52), about 1 inch
　　by 7 inches

1. In a medium bowl, stir together the miso paste, sugar, mirin, vinegar, and mustard until well combined. Add the scallops and toss to coat.

2. Follow the steps for How to Make Gunkanmaki on page 135 to form the nori-wrapped rice balls.

3. Spoon some of the scallops into each boat, and serve immediately.

Cucumber Gunkanmaki with Peanuts and Peanut Sauce

MAKES 8 GUNKANMAKI | PREP TIME: 15 MINUTES

With crisp cucumbers, crunchy peanuts, and a slather of savory peanut sauce, this is a satisfying and delicious vegan sushi option. Fresh grated ginger gives it a kick of brightness.

1 tablespoon natural peanut butter

¾ teaspoon rice vinegar

⅛ teaspoon salt

½ Japanese cucumber, diced small

½ cup roasted, unsalted peanuts, coarsely chopped

1 cup Sushi Rice (page 39)

8 strips Toasted Nori (page 52), about 1 inch by 7 inches

8 cilantro leaves

1 teaspoon finely grated ginger root

1 scallion, thinly sliced

1. In a medium bowl, stir together the peanut butter, vinegar, and salt. Add the cucumber and peanuts, and toss to coat.

2. Follow the steps for How to Make Gunkanmaki on page 135 to form the nori-wrapped rice balls.

3. Spoon some of the cucumbers into each sushi. Garnish each with a cilantro leaf, a dab of grated ginger, and a sprinkling of sliced scallions and serve immediately.

Diced Ginger Eggplant Gunkanmaki

MAKES 8 GUNKANMAKI | PREP TIME: 20 MINUTES | COOK TIME: 12 MINUTES

This quick sauté of gingery eggplant makes a fantastic vegetarian filling for gunkanmaki. If you'd like a bit of spice, add a bit of chile paste or crushed red pepper to the sauce mixture.

1½ teaspoons neutral-flavored oil such as grapeseed or safflower

1½ teaspoons minced ginger

2 scallions, thinly sliced, white and green parts divided

1 small Japanese eggplant, diced

1 tablespoon rice wine vinegar

1 teaspoon soy sauce

1 teaspoon sugar

1 teaspoon cornstarch

1 cup Sushi Rice (page 39)

8 strips Toasted Nori (page 52), about 1 inch by 7 inches

1. In a small skillet over medium-high heat, heat the oil. Add the ginger and the white parts of the scallions and stir once or twice. Add the eggplant and sauté until the eggplant softens, about 5 minutes.

2. In a small bowl, stir together the vinegar, soy sauce, sugar, and cornstarch. Add the mixture to the pan with the eggplant and toss to coat. Bring to a boil. Reduce the heat to medium-low and simmer until the sauce thickens, about 5 minutes more. Remove from the heat and let cool.

3. Follow the steps for How to Make Gunkanmaki on page 135 to form the nori-wrapped rice balls.

4. Spoon some of the eggplant into each sushi. Garnish each with a sprinkling of the reserved green slices of scallions, and serve immediately.

OSHI PRESSED SUSHI

9

Oshi, or pressed sushi, harkens back to the ancient practice of preserving fish by packing it in fermented rice. Before nigiri (finger sushi) was invented in the nineteenth century, all sushi was made in this style with fish, vegetables, and rice layered in a mold and then pressed to form a square block. ⊡ A specially designed oshi mold, called an *oshibako*, is a rectangular box with a removable bottom and lid. It often has slits on the sides for your knife to ensure easy and precise slicing. Traditional oshi molds are made of wood, but plastic molds are available. If you don't have a mold, two small baking pans of the same size will do. Line one pan with foil, layer in the ingredients, top with the second pan (flat-side down), and weight it down for 30 minutes. Unmold the sushi by flipping the pan over, and slice it into pieces for serving.

How to Make OSHI

Oshi (pressed sushi) is made by layering toppings and sushi rice in a mold, and pressing the layers to form a firm block before slicing into bite-size pieces for serving. Whether you lay the toppings or rice first depends on the type of mold you use. Instruction is provided below for molds with and without slits. These recipes make enough for 2 large traditional oshi molds (7 or 8 inches long by 2½ or 3 inches wide by 2 inches deep) or 1 batch made in an 8-by-8-inch by 2-inch baking pan.

INGREDIENTS

Toppings (fish, vegetables, tofu, or eggs)
2 cups Sushi Rice (page 39)
2 cups water mixed with 2 tablespoons rice vinegar, for wetting hands

EQUIPMENT

Oshi mold, with or without slits (separate preparations are given on page 145 and 146)

OR

2 small square or rectangular baking pans, about 2 inches deep, one of them lined with foil (see page 146)

1 Prepare your work area by setting out your toppings and Sushi Rice, as well as the bowl of vinegared water.

2 Trim the fish or other toppings so that they can be placed in the mold in a single layer. Blot the toppings dry with paper towels.

Depending on which mold you are using, continue steps 3 through 7 on page 145 or 146.

FOR A MOLD WITH SLITS

3 Dip your hands in the bowl of vinegared water, and then spread the rice evenly across the bottom of the mold. Press it down uniformly with the lid, and then remove the lid.

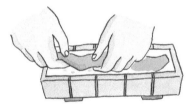

4 Cover the rice in a single layer with the toppings noted in the individual recipe. Press down with the lid again, and then remove it.

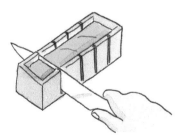

5 Wet a sharp knife with water and align the knife in the first of the mold's slits, then proceed to slice and repeat with each of the slits.

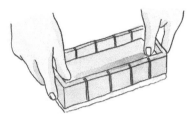

6 To unmold the sushi, place the lid on top again, and then press down on it while lifting up the sides of the mold.

7 Wet your knife again and finish slicing through each piece now that the oshi has been unmolded.

145

OSHI

continued ▶

FOR A MOLD WITHOUT SLITS OR A BAKING PAN

3 Line the bottom of the mold with the toppings noted in the individual recipe. The toppings should cover the entire bottom of the mold.

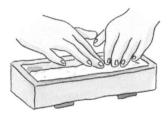

4 Dip your hands in the bowl of vinegared water. Then add a layer of sushi rice over the toppings so that the mold is about two-thirds full. With your fingers, press the rice down in an even layer. Place a clean lid on top of the rice (or place the second baking pan on top), and press down firmly for a good 10 to 20 seconds.

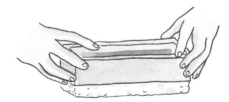

5 If you have an oshi mold, keep your thumbs on the lid of the mold while lifting off the sides of the wooden frame.

6 Carefully flip the mold over onto a cutting board so that the toppings are in top. Remove the base of the mold.

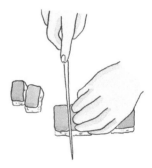

7 Wet a sharp knife with water and then slice individual pieces. If you are making the oshi in advance, wrap the block of sushi tightly in plastic wrap and store in a cool spot (not in the refrigerator) until ready to slice and serve.

Cured Mackerel Oshi

MAKES ABOUT 12 PIECES |
PREP TIME: 15 MINUTES, PLUS 30 MINUTES TO SIT AND 24 HOURS TO MARINATE

In Japan, mackerel is always served cooked or cured. Curing the fish in salt (or sometimes sugar) and vinegar serves to both kill any bacteria and cut the oiliness and strong flavor of the fish. Cured mackerel is a common topping used for oshi. Here the cured mackerel is made the same way it is made for Marinated Mackerel Sashimi (page 67).

2 mackerel fillets, about 4 ounces each, skinned
1 tablespoon plus 1 teaspoon salt, divided
1½ cups unseasoned rice vinegar
1½ tablespoons sugar
1 tablespoon mirin
2 cups Sushi Rice (page 39)

1. Sprinkle the fillets on both sides with the 1 tablespoon of salt. In a glass baking dish or other nonreactive dish wide enough to hold the fish in a single layer, place the fillets. Cover and let sit for 30 minutes.

2. Rinse the fillets gently under cold water to remove the salt. Pat dry. Drain any liquid that has accumulated in the baking dish.

3. In the drained baking dish, combine the vinegar, sugar, mirin, and remaining 1 teaspoon of salt. Stir until the sugar is dissolved. Place the fish in the baking dish. Cover and refrigerate for at least 24 hours.

4. Remove the fish from the marinade and pat dry.

5. Follow the instructions for How to Make Oshi on page 144, beginning by arranging the cured mackerel in the mold in a single layer.

6. Add the layer of rice, place the lid of the mold on top, and press to compact the rice. Unmold the sushi, slice into rectangular pieces about 1½ by 2 inches, and serve immediately.

Yellowtail Oshi with Chile-Daikon Relish

MAKES ABOUT 12 PIECES | PREP TIME: 15 MINUTES, PLUS 30 MINUTES TO SIT

The mild but rich flavor of yellowtail works perfectly with the spicy crunch of Chile Daikon Relish (page 54). You could substitute another white fish if you like, such as halibut.

8 ounces yellowtail fillet
Chile-Daikon Relish (page 54)
2 cups Sushi Rice (page 39)

1. Follow the instructions for How to Make Oshi on page 144, beginning by arranging the yellowtail fillet in the mold in a single layer.

2. Add a layer of the Chile-Daikon Relish and then a layer of rice.

3. Place the lid of the mold on top, and press to compact the rice.

4. After 30 minutes, unmold the sushi, slice into rectangular pieces about 1½ by 2 inches, and serve immediately.

Eel Oshi

MAKES ABOUT 12 PIECES | PREP TIME: 15 MINUTES, PLUS 30 MINUTES TO SIT | COOK TIME: 2 MINUTES

Freshwater eel (unagi) is a rich, oily fish that is best served grilled or broiled. You can buy it already cooked and frozen in Japanese markets. Eel Sauce (page 59) is a sweet soy-based glaze that perfectly complements the rich fish.

8 ounces cooked eel fillet

Eel Sauce (page 59), warmed in a saucepan on the stove top or in the microwave

2 cups Sushi Rice (page 39)

1. Preheat the broiler to high.

2. On a baking sheet, brush the eel with some of the Eel Sauce. Broil for about 2 minutes, until the sauce begins to bubble.

3. Follow the instructions for How to Make Oshi on page 144, beginning by arranging the eel in the mold in a single layer.

4. Add a layer of rice.

5. Place the lid of the mold on top, and press to compact the rice.

6. After 30 minutes, unmold the sushi and slice into rectangular pieces about 1½ by 2 inches. Brush the tops of the sushi pieces with sauce, and serve immediately.

Smoked Salmon Oshi with Lemon

MAKES ABOUT 12 PIECES | PREP TIME: 15 MINUTES, PLUS 30 MINUTES TO SIT

Smoked salmon oshi is an easy sushi to make at home. The pressing technique is easy to master, and you can buy good-quality smoked salmon in most supermarkets. This version is brightened with finely grated lemon zest and a squeeze of lemon juice.

8 ounces sliced smoked salmon
2 cups Sushi Rice (page 39)
1 lemon, scrubbed

1. Follow the instructions for How to Make Oshi on page 144, beginning by arranging the smoked salmon in the mold in a single layer.

2. Using a fine-toothed zester, zest the lemon directly over the salmon. Add a layer of rice.

3. Place the lid of the mold on top, and press to compact the rice.

4. After 30 minutes, unmold the sushi, squeeze a bit of lemon juice over the top, and slice into rectangular pieces about 1½ by 2 inches. Serve immediately.

Soy-Cured Beet Oshi with Avocado

MAKES ABOUT 12 PIECES | PREP TIME: 20 MINUTES, PLUS 2 HOURS TO MARINATE AND 30 MINUTES TO SIT | COOK TIME: 1 HOUR

Tender roasted beets look similar to raw tuna. Arranged with bright green avocado, the effect is stunning. Roasting the beets deepens their flavor, but if you don't have time, you could quarter them and steam them for about 15 minutes or so until they are tender.

2 medium beets, trimmed
¼ cup soy sauce, plus extra for serving
¼ cup water
1 medium avocado, thinly sliced
2 cups Sushi Rice (page 39)

1. Preheat the oven to 400ºF.

2. Wrap the beets in aluminum foil, and place them on a baking sheet. Bake for about 1 hour, until the beets are easily pierced with a fork. Remove from the oven and let cool. Once cool enough to handle, slip off the skins and slice into pieces about ⅛-inch thick and 1½ inches wide.

3. In a large bowl, whisk together the soy sauce and water. Add the beets and toss to coat. Cover and refrigerate for at least 2 hours.

4. Remove the beets from the marinade, rinse, and pat dry.

5. Follow the instructions for How to Make Oshi on page 144, beginning by arranging the beets and avocado in alternating diagonal stripes.

6. Add a layer of rice.

7. Place the lid of the mold on top, and press to compact the rice.

8. After 30 minutes, unmold the sushi and slice into rectangular pieces about 1½ by 2 inches. Serve immediately.

SOUPS AND SALADS

10

Japanese meals, including sushi meals, are rarely single-serving affairs. They are usually made up of many different dishes, little bites of this and that, something hot, something cold, something crunchy, something creamy—feeding the senses when sitting down to eat is as important as nourishing the body. Which means, just about every meal includes soup and salad. ▣ Soups can be light: clear dashi or broth with vegetables or tofu. They can also be hearty: stews filled with seafood, meat, eggs, or noodles. Salads can be soft or crunchy and include raw vegetable salads with miso dressing, cooked vegetable salads, seaweed salads, or piquant quick-pickled vegetables. You'll want to choose at least one of the savory or refreshing recipes in this chapter to offer along with the sushi and sashimi you serve to your family and friends, or prepare a soup and salad to create a meal by themselves.

Miso Soup
with Mushrooms and Tofu

SERVES 4 | PREP TIME: 5 MINUTES | COOK TIME: 10 MINUTES

Dashi is a Japanese-style stock made with bonito flakes (thinly shaved flakes of dried, smoked tuna) and kombu (dried kelp). Vegetarian dashi is made with just kombu. If you don't have a batch of dashi made, you can use instant dashi packets, available at Japanese markets, or substitute vegetable broth.

4 cups Stock (page 55)

6 ounces tofu, cubed

4 ounces fresh shiitake mushrooms, sliced

2 cups leafy greens, such as bok choy or kale, julienned

¼ cup miso paste

2 scallions, thinly sliced

1. In a medium saucepan over medium-high heat, bring the stock to a boil. Add the tofu, mushrooms, and greens and return to a boil. Reduce the heat and simmer for about 5 minutes, until the vegetables are tender.

2. In a heat-proof bowl or glass measuring cup, stir together the miso paste and about ½ cup of the hot broth to combine well. Add the mixture to the soup, and stir. Serve immediately, garnished with the scallions.

Chawanmushi

SERVES 4 | PREP TIME: 5 MINUTES | COOK TIME: 15 MINUTES

Chawanmushi is a savory egg custard. Like the Miso Soup with Mushrooms and Tofu (opposite page), it is also made with dashi (page 55), or Japanese stock. The dashi and eggs are steamed together, along with other savory ingredients, including meat and vegetables, and the custard forms a creamy layer over the broth. Traditionally chawanmushi is made in ceramic cups with lids, but you can use ramekins covered with foil instead.

3 eggs

2 cups Stock (page 55)

½ teaspoon salt

1 teaspoon soy sauce

1 teaspoon sugar

1 teaspoon sake

4 ounces boneless, skinless chicken thigh, cut into bite-size pieces (optional)

4 shiitake mushrooms, stemmed and sliced

1. In a medium bowl, lightly beat the eggs, being careful not to incorporate too much air into them. Add the stock, salt, soy sauce, sugar, and sake, and beat to mix. Pass the mixture through a fine-mesh sieve.

2. Fill a large pot fitted with a wide, flat steamer with a few inches of water and bring to a boil.

3. Divide the custard, chicken (if using), and mushrooms evenly among 4 (6-ounce) ramekins or custard cups. Cover the ramekins with foil, and place them on the steamer over the boiling water. Cover the pot and steam for about 15 minutes. The custard should be fully set. Serve hot.

Soba Noodle and Spinach Soup in Ginger Broth

SERVES 4 | PREP TIME: 10 MINUTES | COOK TIME: 10 MINUTES

Soba noodles, made from buckwheat flour, are both heartier and more flavorful than ramen. They transform this ginger-spiked, 10-minute soup into a hearty first course. To make it a meal, add diced chicken or tofu or whole shrimp.

1 teaspoon sesame oil

1 teaspoon neutral-flavored oil such as grapeseed or safflower

½ cup sliced shiitake mushrooms

1 shallot, thinly sliced

1½ teaspoons finely grated fresh ginger

4 cups reduced-sodium chicken broth

1 tablespoon sake or mirin

1 tablespoon soy sauce

1½ teaspoons rice vinegar

1 tablespoon miso paste

½ cup chopped spinach leaves

1 scallion, sliced thin

4 ounces dried soba noodles, cooked according to package directions

1. In a medium stockpot or large saucepan over medium heat, heat the sesame oil and neutral-flavored oil. Add the mushrooms, shallot, and ginger and cook, stirring frequently, for about 3 to 5 minutes, until the vegetables soften and begin to brown.

2. Add the broth, sake, soy sauce, and vinegar and bring to a boil. Reduce the heat to medium-low and simmer for 5 minutes. Just before serving, stir in the miso paste, spinach, and scallions.

3. Divide the noodles among four soup bowls, and ladle the soup over them. Serve hot.

Green Salad with Creamy Miso Dressing

SERVES 4 | PREP TIME: 10 MINUTES

This quick dressing tastes remarkably similar to that served in many Japanese restaurants. This crunchy salad is a perfect accompaniment to sushi or sashimi, but it would also be at home with grilled steak or fish.

FOR THE DRESSING

¼ cup white or yellow miso paste

2½ tablespoons water

2 tablespoons sugar

1½ tablespoons rice wine vinegar

1 teaspoon soy sauce

⅛ teaspoon kosher salt

1 tablespoon neutral-flavored oil such as grapeseed or safflower

½ teaspoon sesame oil

FOR THE SALAD

5 ounces salad greens

1 Japanese cucumber, thinly sliced

1 medium carrot, grated on the wide holes of a box grater

To make the dressing

1. In a small bowl, whisk together the miso paste, water, sugar, vinegar, soy sauce, and salt to combine well.

2. While whisking, slowly add the neutral-flavored oil and sesame oil, until the dressing is thick, creamy, and well combined.

To make the salad

1. In a medium salad bowl, toss together the salad greens, cucumber, and carrot.

2. Add the dressing and toss gently until the vegetables are well coated. Serve immediately.

Chilled Spinach with Sesame Dressing

SERVES 4 | PREPARATION TIME: 15 MINUTES | COOK TIME: 1 MINUTE

This delicate salad is full of intense sesame flavor. Toasted sesame seeds are ground to a paste to make the sauce, which is then tossed with blanched spinach. Serve it alongside sushi or sashimi, or enjoy it with a grilled steak.

FOR THE DRESSING

3 tablespoons white sesame seeds
1½ tablespoons soy sauce
1 tablespoon sugar
1 teaspoon mirin

FOR THE SALAD

1 bunch (about 8 ounces) spinach
Pinch salt

To make the dressing

1. In a small skillet over medium-high heat, toast the sesame seeds, shaking the pan frequently, until the seeds become fragrant and begin to pop, about 1 to 2 minutes. Remove the seeds from the heat immediately.

2. Transfer the seeds to a food processor and pulse into a paste. Transfer the sesame paste to a small bowl and whisk together with the soy sauce, sugar, and mirin to make the dressing.

To make the salad

1. Prepare a large bowl of ice water. In a large pot over medium-high heat, bring enough lightly salted water to cover the spinach to a boil. Add the spinach and cook for about 1 minute, until the spinach is wilted. Drain the spinach and transfer to the ice water bath.

2. When the spinach is cool, remove it from the water and drain well, squeezing out any excess water.

3. In a medium bowl, toss the spinach with the sesame dressing. Cover and chill until ready to serve.

Cabbage Salad with Miso-Lime Dressing

SERVES 4 | PREP TIME: 10 MINUTES | COOK TIME: 1 MINUTE

This light, citrusy raw vegetable salad is refreshing alongside heavier dishes like tempura or grilled eel, but it also makes a nice crunchy counterpoint to any sushi or sashimi dish. Shred the cabbage in a food processor, and you can have this dish on the table in minutes.

1 tablespoon black sesame seeds
1 tablespoon white or yellow miso paste
2 tablespoons soy sauce
Juice and zest of 1 lime
2 teaspoons unseasoned rice wine vinegar
1 teaspoon sesame oil
¼ cup neutral-flavored oil such as grapeseed or safflower
6 cups thinly shredded green cabbage

1. In a small skillet over medium-high heat, toast the sesame seeds, shaking the pan frequently, until the seeds become fragrant and begin to pop, about 1 minute. Remove the seeds from the pan and set aside.

2. In a large salad bowl, whisk together the miso paste, soy sauce, lime juice and zest, and vinegar, slowly adding the sesame oil and the neutral-flavored oil while whisking. Continue whisking until the dressing is well combined and emulsified.

3. Add the cabbage to the bowl, and toss to coat well with the dressing. Garnish with the toasted sesame seeds, and serve immediately.

GLOSSARY

Abura age: Deep-fried tofu

Ahi: Yellowfin tuna

Akamiso: Red miso

Ama ebi: Raw shrimp

Anago: Saltwater eel

Asazuke: Thinly sliced Japanese cucumbers quickly pickled in a vinegar and sugar brine

Awasemiso: Mixed miso

Beni shoga: Red ginger pickled in *umeboshi* brine (made from ume plums)

Bonito flakes: Thinly shaved flakes of dried, smoked tuna

Chirashi: "Scattered sushi," sashimi, and other ingredients arranged over a bowl of sushi rice

Daiginjo or Junmai-daigingo: The highest grade of sake

Daikon: Japanese white radish

Dashi: Japanese broth

Ebi: Shrimp

Futomaki: Big roll

Gari: Pickled ginger

Geta: A wooden plank for serving sushi

Ginjo or Junmai-gingo: Super-premium sake

Gunkan: Battleship

Gunkanmaki: Battleship rolls

Hamachi: Yellowtail

Hangiri: A wide, flat-bottomed wooden bowl used to make sushi rice

Hirame: Halibut

Honjozu or Junmai-honjozu: Premium sake

Hosomaki: Thin roll

Hotate: Scallop

Ikura: Salmon roe

Inari-zushi: A type of sushi in which vinegared rice and other ingredients are stuffed into a pouch made from deep-fried tofu (abura age)

Japonica rice: Japanese-style short-grain white rice

Junmai-shu: Table sake

Kaiten-zushi: Sushi served on a conveyer belt

Kaiware: Daikon radish sprouts

Kampyo: Dried gourd

Katana: Samurai sword

Kombu: Dried kelp

Maguro: Bluefin tuna

Maki: Rolled sushi

Makisu: A bamboo sushi rolling mat

Masago: Capelin roe

Meshi: Rice

Mirin: Sweet rice wine

Miso: A paste made from fermented soybean

Namazake: Unpasteurized or "fresh" sake

Nare-zushi: The earliest form of sushi, which was fish preserved in lacto-fermented rice

Negi: Scallions

Nigiri: Hand-formed sushi

Nigori: Unfiltered sake

Nori: Thin sheets of dried seaweed

Norimaki: Sushi rolls with nori on the outside

Ochazuke wakame: Seasoning mix made of dried seaweed and crispy rice balls, also called wakame chazuke

Oshi: Pressed sushi

Oshibako: Mold for making oshi

Oshinko: A crunchy pickled daikon (Japanese radish) that takes on a bright yellow hue from the bacterium *Bacillus subtilis* during rice-bran fermentation and the addition of persimmon peels, nasturtium flowers, or other colorings. Also known as Takuan.

Saba: Mackerel

Sake: Rice wine or salmon

Santoku knife: A Japanese all-purpose knife with very sharp blades featuring a dimpled pattern that causes sticky foods to release more easily

Shamoji: A wooden rice paddle

Shibazuke: Cucumbers and eggplant brined in salt and red shiso

Shime saba: Marinated mackerel

Shiromiso: White miso

Shiso: A fresh herb in the mint family; also called perilla leaf

Su: Vinegar

Sumeshi: Vinagared rice

Surimi: Crab sticks; an imitation crab made of processed white fish flesh shaped and colored to resemble snow crab or Japanese spider crab legs

Sushi-ya: Sushi restaurant

Tai: Snapper

Tamago or Tamagoyaki: Japanese rolled omelet

Temaki: Hand-rolled sushi

Temari: Rice balls

Tobiko: Flying fish roe

Tsukemono: Pickles

Umeboshi: Plums pickled in salt and red shiso

Unagi: Freshwater eel

Unagidon: A rice bowl topped with cooked unagi

Uramaki: Inside-out sushi rolls (with rice on the outside)

Wasabi: Japanese horseradish

Zuke: Marinated or cured

RESOURCES

With the ever-growing popularity of sushi, both in the United States and around the world, it gets easier and easier to find the tools and resources you need to make sushi at home. Even if you don't have access to a Japanese market, it's easy to find books, cooking utensils, and ingredients for making homemade sushi.

BOOKS

Berber, Kamiko, and Hiroki Takemura. *Sushi: Taste and Technique*. New York, NY: Dorling Kindersley, LTD., 2002.

Imatani, Aya. *Sushi: The Beginner's Guide*. Watertown, MA: Imagine Publishing, 2009.

Kawasumi, Ken. *The Encyclopedia of Sushi Rolls*. Tokyo, Japan: Graph-sha LTD., 2001.

Kazuko, Emi. *Easy Sushi*. New York, NY: Ryland Peters & Small, 2000.

Sone, Hiro, and Lissa Doumani. *A Visual Guide to Sushi-Making at Home*. San Francisco, CA: Chronicle Books, 2014.

Strada, Judy, and Mineko Takane Moreno. *Sushi for Dummies*. Indianapolis, IN: Wiley Publishing, Inc., 2004.

ONLINE RESOURCES

Amazon
amazon.com

Amazon allows numerous Japanese food merchants to sell their products through its platform. On amazon.com, you can find ingredients from kombu to nori, miso, wasabi paste, and yuzu juice. You'll also find tools like sushi mats, wooden rice bowls, and oshi molds.

Asian Food Grocer
asianfoodgrocer.com

This online store carries ingredients from all over Asia, including Japan, but they also stock a full range of cooking supplies, including everything you need to make sushi, such as sushi mats and molds, rice bowls, Japanese knives, and more. Orders are shipped quickly from their San Francisco warehouse.

JapanSuper.com

This online market carries all things Japanese—seaweed, sauces, miso paste, noodles, fresh produce, fish cakes, fish roe, and pickles. Orders are processed within 24 hours and arrive in one to five days.

Marukai eStore
marukaiestore.com

This well-stocked virtual Japanese market carries rice, nori, sauces, seasonings, and pickles as well as kitchenware and rice cookers.

Mitsuwa Marketplace
mitsuwa.com

With brick-and-mortar store locations across the United States, Mitsuwa's e-store is nearly as convenient as having a Japanese market around the corner. They carry every sort of Japanese ingredient you could want, including fresh and frozen produce, meat, and fish. Next-day shipping is available.

Pike Place Fish Market
pikeplacefish.com

The famous Seattle fishmonger offers online shopping and overnight shipping on their top-quality sustainable seafood.

Vital Choice
vitalchoice.com

This website sells wild-caught, sustainably harvested seafood. The seafood is flash frozen immediately after being caught and shipped directly to consumers. They carry everything from wild-caught shrimp and scallops to tuna, cod, salmon, and more. Seafood orders are shipped via 2- or 3-day UPS.

INDEX